# Coaching
from **A** to **Z**
# and Back Again

**More coaching and mentoring titles from Critical Publishing:**

Coaching Young People for Leadership
by Mark Jamieson
978-1-915080-47-9

Dial M for Mentor:
Critical Reflections on Mentoring for Coaches, Educators and Trainers
by Jonathan Gravells and Susan Wallace
978-1-909330-00-9

Non-directive Coaching:
Attitudes, Approaches and Applications
by Bob Thomson
978-1-909330-57-3

To order our books please go to our website www.criticalpublishing.com or contact our distributor Ingram Publisher Services, telephone 01752 202301 or email IPSUK.orders@ingramcontent.com. Details of bulk order discounts can be found at www.criticalpublishing.com/delivery-information.

Our titles are also available in electronic format: for individual use via our website and for libraries and other institutions from all the major ebook platforms.

CRITICAL
PUBLISHING

# Coaching
## from A to Z
# and Back Again

"

# 52 ideas,
## tools and models
### for **great**
# coaching
# conversations

"

## BOB THOMSON

First published in 2023 by Critical Publishing Ltd

British Library Cataloguing in Publication Data
A CIP record for this book is available from the British Library

ISBN: 978-1-915080-29-5

This book is also available in the following e-book formats:
EPUB ISBN: 978-1-915080-30-1
Adobe e-book ISBN: 978-1-915080-31-8

Cover design by Out of House Limited
Text design by Greensplash
Project management by Newgen Publishing UK
Printed and bound in Great Britain by 4edge, Essex

Critical Publishing
3 Connaught Road
St Albans
AL3 5RX

www.criticalpublishing.com

Printed on FSC accredited paper

# CONTENTS

## About the author

Bob Thomson is a professor at Warwick Business School. He is an experienced coach, supervisor and management development professional, accredited as a coach and supervisor by the European Mentoring and Coaching Council. He is also a qualified and experienced mediator. He is the author of a number of books on coaching and is the editor of Critical Publishing's series of books on mental well-being in the workplace, *Business in Mind*.

He can be contacted by email at bob.thomson@wbs.ac.uk

## Introduction

In this book, I set out a variety of ideas that invite you to reflect upon and develop your coaching skills and practice. I explore models and frameworks that I personally draw upon in my work as a coach, supervisor and mediator. I also share some personal reflections and experiences. I hope that you will find many of the topics covered interesting and, more importantly, useful.

I worked in management development in the gas industry for 17 years before joining the University of Warwick in 2005, first in an internal learning and development role and then as an academic at Warwick Business School. Coaching is my main professional interest – working as a coach, helping people learn how to coach, acting as a supervisor for other coaches and writing about coaching. I find that these activities are mutually reinforcing.

My approach to coaching, and to learning and development, rests on two important foundations. The first is the ideas of Carl Rogers, who established a person-centred approach to therapy and counselling. I describe my practice as a coach as primarily non-directive. The second is the ideas of David Kolb on learning from experience and the experiential learning cycle. I draw on both of these at various points throughout the book.

I had the very good fortune to learn about coaching on the first course run by Myles Downey and Jane Meyler at the School of Coaching. I was then privileged to run a coaching programme for several years for managers in Transco, the gas pipeline company, in partnership with John Whitmore and his colleagues. The ideas of Downey and Whitmore have also greatly influenced my approach to coaching.

The 52 chapters which follow – from A to Z and back again – are all around 1000 words in length. I've included an exercise at the end of each chapter – generally either a reflective task or a link to a video or article. I often quote other writers on coaching, and each chapter contains the appropriate references to the original sources.

The order of the chapters was determined by the alphabet. While I included some basic ideas in earlier chapters, the various chapters don't follow one another. Some readers may choose to read each chapter in turn, while others may wish to select the topics that interest them most. I enjoyed writing to this format, and I hope that you enjoy reading from it too.

Finally, I'd like to thank Julia Morris and her colleagues at Critical Publishing, Lizzie Evans of Newgen Publishing, and Victoria Chow and Emma Wiggin for their practical support and guidance in the production of the book.

*Bob Thomson*

# From A to Z ...

# Chapter 1: A

## AWARENESS + RESPONSIBILITY = PERFORMANCE

In the late 1990s, when I was working as the Learning and Development Manager at the gas pipeline company Transco, I went out to tender for a coaching skills programme for the company's managers. The tender for the programme, which involved a three-day workshop followed sometime later by a two-day workshop, was won by John Whitmore's firm, Performance Consultants.

Whitmore played a leading role in the development of coaching in Britain. His book, *Coaching for Performance*, first published in 1992, is still in print, now in its fifth edition. One of the smartest things I ever did was to say to John and his colleagues that I would deliver the programme alongside them. They initially said no, but I insisted. So, for the next five years or so I worked with John and others to facilitate the delivery of the programme. I had the pleasure not only of co-facilitating but also having some great conversations over dinner with John and his colleagues, David Hemery, David Whitaker and Sue Slocombe.

I had some firm views on the power of experiential learning, and I believe that my approach coupled with the deep knowledge of coaching that John and his colleagues possessed made for a great programme. One of the central ideas was captured in the equation:

Awareness + responsibility = performance

John Whitmore reflects this in his book when he writes that *'Building AWARENESS and RESPONSIBILITY is the essence of good coaching'* (Whitmore, 2002). The premise is that someone who has good awareness – of the situation and perhaps the wider context, of themselves and their hopes and fears, of relevant constraints, etc – and who takes responsibility – that is, responsibility for taking appropriate action – will perform, whatever performance means in the situation (it might be making a sales call, managing a team, finishing a report or hitting a tennis or golf ball, etc). Someone who is *aware* of what they need to do and who takes *responsibility* will *perform*.

Over the years I have reused many of the ideas and some of the exercises from that original programme for Transco managers. In sharing the equation with participants on a coaching skills programme, I highlight that a useful way of thinking about what you are doing when you ask a question in a coaching conversation is that the question is designed either to raise the client's awareness or to encourage them to take responsibility for action – or perhaps both.

John Whitmore used to add a line during the workshops which I find both amusing and thought-provoking. He'd say: *'Awareness without responsibility is just whingeing.'* So, for instance, someone who knows a lot about what's wrong in their department, but who's doing nothing to improve things, is just whingeing.

In inviting participants to reflect on this idea, I have occasionally been challenged, which has led me to modify the equation somewhat. I think the equation misses two important points. First, someone might be very aware of their situation and also genuinely wish to improve it, but fear or lack of confidence prevents them from taking action. I think that lack of confidence is a crucial factor in many coaching conversations. Second, someone may lack the capability to take effective action, either because they personally lack the necessary skill or knowledge, or because they do not have the resources (such as a budget or staff) that are required. Thus, you might modify the equation to read:

$$\text{Awareness + responsibility + confidence + capability = performance}$$

It's not as elegant as the original. And the simpler focus on raising awareness and encouraging responsibility will take you very far in your coaching conversations.

My own approach to coaching and to helping people learn how to coach owes much to listening to and working with Whitmore and his colleagues on those workshops. When I compiled the index for my first book on coaching, *Don't Just Do Something, Sit There*, which was published in 2009, I realised that I'd made 12 separate references to Whitmore. His ideas permeate the text of this book, too. One of the ideas which he popularised in his book (although he didn't create it himself) is the GROW model, which we explore in a later chapter. This is probably the most well-known and used framework for structuring a coaching conversation, at least in a British context. A brief summary of the GROW model reflects the centrality of awareness and responsibility:

**G**oal        What are you trying to achieve?

**R**eality     What is currently going on?

**O**ptions     What might you do?

**W**ill        What will you do?

You might think of exploring the client's Goal, Reality and Options as being mainly about raising awareness, while helping them to explore their Options and Will is about encouraging responsibility.

I find that most people who have attended a coaching skills programme have some recollection of the GROW framework. It's a useful mnemonic, but it's merely one way of structuring a conversation. Fewer of them remember that building awareness and responsibility is a much more fundamental notion, which gets to the heart of effective coaching. For example, in choosing what question to ask next or what exercise to propose, it's useful to check mentally if your choice is likely to raise the client's awareness or encourage them to take responsibility for action. If it's unlikely to do either, do something else. As an illustration, it can be easy to fall into the trap of gathering lots of information about the organisation chart that features the client. Sometimes you need to know a little of this to understand their context, but gathering lots of data that the client already knows is unlikely to help them.

**READING**

Follow this link to see a range of quotes from John Whitmore that illustrate well his philosophy of coaching: www. goodreads.com/author/quotes/121298.John_Whitmore

## References

Thomson, B (2009) *Don't Just Do Something, Sit There: An Introduction to Non-directive Coaching*. Oxford: Chandos Publishing.

Whitmore, J (2002) *Coaching for Performance: The Principles of Coaching and Leadership*. London: Nicholas Brealey.

# Chapter 2: B

## BOUNDARIES

In working as a coach, it is very important to be clear in your own mind what your role is. A vital aspect of this is how directive or non-directive you choose to be. In the chapter *'Don't Just Do Something, Sit There'*, we'll look at a spectrum of behaviours from being directive to being non-directive. Operating at the directive end, a coach might give advice, offer guidance, make suggestions or even give instructions. At the non-directive end, a coach will draw on the key conversational skills of listening to understand, asking open questions and playing back their understanding to the client. I believe that it's vital that you are clear where you stand on this spectrum, both in an overall, philosophical sense and in the moment when you decide what to say or do next in the middle of a coaching session.

Another aspect on which it is important to be clear relates to the boundaries of how you view your role as a coach. I think there are two aspects here. The first is a boundary of *competence*. So, for example, I am a coach, not a counsellor. I think there is considerable overlap between these two activities, and the skill of empathic listening is the foundation of both. In the safety of a sound coaching relationship, a client may touch on some highly emotional topics, such as relationships or childhood experiences. This may provide important context for the challenges that they are bringing to coaching. So, while I will give the client space to mention these, I won't attempt to explore them in depth – that's beyond my role and my competence.

To give an actual example from my experience as an internal coach at the University of Warwick, I worked over a period of months with a member of staff who had substantial challenges in her relationship with her line manager. In exploring how she handled this, she did talk about her childhood and her difficulties in being assertive, often tearfully. We explored together whether or not she needed to see a counsellor to work through these deeper issues, and the client chose to do this. I continued to help her to address how she would behave at work, particularly in relation to her manager, while she met a counsellor to explore deeper, psychological issues.

My experience with this particular client helps me to crystallise a rule of thumb that I find useful. In my practice as a coach, it's okay if there are tears occasionally in the coaching room, but if there are tears regularly then this strongly suggests that the client needs to see a counsellor or therapist – perhaps instead of, or perhaps as well as, seeing me as their coach.

The example also highlights the importance of explicitly discussing with the client what is happening, and raising the possibility that they need further or different support. This is reflected in the following sentence from the Global Code of Ethics for Coaches, Mentors, and Supervisors (which has been agreed by a number of leading coaching bodies, including the Association for Coaching and the European Mentoring and Coaching Council):

> *Members will operate within the limit of their professional competence. Members should refer the client to a more experienced or suitably qualified practicing member where appropriate.*
>
> (Global Code of Ethics, 2021, p 9)

I would add that referral may be to someone in a different profession, not only a more experienced coach. I do have some concerns about the word *refer*. This may give the impression that the coach will contact someone else on the client's behalf. While this sometimes might be appropriate, I think that it's generally the responsibility of the client to make contact with another professional whose support they require. I may help the client to think through some possibilities – for instance, what type of counsellor might be most suitable – but I leave the action to follow this up with the client.

The second type of boundary is one of *appropriateness*. For example, acting as an internal coach within my organisation, it's not appropriate for me to explore marital problems that are troubling a fellow member of staff – even if I was trained to do so. Similarly, it wouldn't be appropriate for me to act as a financial adviser with a work colleague, even if I were qualified to do so (which, again, I'm not!).

It is useful to mention the issue of boundaries in an initial contracting session with a new client. The reality of what this actually means in practice might not become clear until a later session. If it does emerge as an issue, it's important that you as the coach raise it explicitly and, if appropriate, discuss with the client how they might find a suitable person to support them.

In my role as the supervisor of the work of other coaches, there are times when a supervisee brings an issue which raises this question of boundaries. To give an illustration from my own supervision practice, one of my supervisees is an experienced coach who was formerly a very successful senior manager in a number of commercial businesses. In his current practice as an executive coach, he often has strong views on what a client needs to do for the success of their business. One of the things I do in our supervision sessions is to help him clarify when he is acting as a primarily non-directive coach, when he is acting in effect as a mentor and when he is acting as an organisational consultant. The roles overlap, but he finds it helpful to identify clearly what is the *appropriate* role for him to take – and why – with a client that he's working with. As an experienced former executive, he is *competent* to take on the role of mentor or consultant, and this may also be *appropriate* in much of his work.

One of the roles I have at Warwick Business School is as a senior tutor for half of our final year undergraduates. In speaking with students about challenging circumstances – sadly, often mental health issues – that are affecting their studies, I find it useful to draw on coaching skills, especially listening skills, to help me understand their situation. But I'm not their coach – there are often times when I will give specific advice to a student on what they need to do in order to, for example, formally apply for mitigating circumstances to be considered by an exam board. And neither am I a counsellor, so I will often recommend that a student contacts the Student Well-being Services team who can support them professionally in this regard. Clarity on role and boundaries is vital.

> **REFLECTIVE TASK**
>
> Think about your own practice as a coach, or perhaps one of the roles that you play as part of your job.
>
> - What boundaries of *competence* are relevant?
> - What boundaries of *appropriateness* are relevant?

## Reference

Global Code of Ethics (2021) Global Code of Ethics for Coaches, Mentors, and Supervisors. [online] Available at: https://emccuk.org/Common/Uploaded%20files/Policies/Global_Code_of_Ethics_EN_v3.pdf (accessed 7 September 2022).

# Chapter 3: C

## CULTURE

In my role at Warwick Business School, I lead a module on our full-time MBA programme called LeadershipPlus. The module aims to help participants to develop their personal effectiveness, their ability to work with others and their leadership and management skills. It is a distinctive module, very different from the other modules on the MBA. It is highly experiential, and invites each student to think deeply about themselves, what they stand for and how they wish to behave as a manager when they return to the world of work after their MBA. The students come from all corners of the globe – it is a truly international cohort. Most of them value the module highly, while a few hate it and would much prefer a more academic exploration of leadership.

I am very conscious that the ethos of the module reflects a Western, perhaps Anglo-Saxon, view of the world. To give one illustration, one of the five workshops that make up the module is about how to have a courageous conversation, exploring honestly and authentically what you'd really like to say. We are suggesting that the ability to speak openly and to give constructive feedback to others, including perhaps your boss, is valuable. I realise, however, that in many parts of the world, the cultural norms are very different from those in the UK. Challenging one's boss simply isn't what one does in many cultures (including some organisational cultures in Britain, too).

While acknowledging that we're not reflecting the cultural diversity of the students in our approach, I simply don't think it's possible to give equal weight to all the different perspectives that might be possible. I take some reassurance from the fact that the students have chosen to come to the UK to study and learn.

In a similar way, the idea of coaching that I'm sharing with you in this book reflects a British view of the world. (It also reflects my own preferences and prejudices, which come through at various points in the text.) This raises the question of how far can the ideas of coaching that we're exploring in this book be adopted – or adapted – for use in other cultures.

A few years ago, I supervised the dissertation of Will Percy, a student on Warwick Business School's distance learning MBA. Will is British, lived and worked in schools in China for 15 years, and married a Chinese woman. His dissertation explored how to use coaching with young Chinese teachers working in an international school in China. Will used the same definition of coaching that I'm using in this book (which I'll share in the next chapter).

Chinese society is far more hierarchical than British society. This suggests that a more directive approach to coaching, one where the coach is expected to be more senior and a source of wisdom, might be appropriate. While recognising this, Will suggested that a coach operating in a Chinese context needed to be able to move between the directive and non-directive ends of the spectrum.

*Saving face* is very important in China, where confrontation is often avoided and negative feedback is given indirectly. When Will interviewed the two coaches who had worked with the young Chinese teachers, they made the following points that seem very relevant for anyone thinking of coaching in a society such as China.

- Relationships took longer than usual to form, although they did become deep and often discussed personal issues.
- Listening was intensive and energy draining, given the need to listen for what was not being said.
- Follow-up activities were often not completed by the coachees, frequently because a superior or colleague had not

played their part. The coachees in turn did not want to speak badly of their superior or colleague, or admit they hadn't carried out the action.
- Playback and feedback were initially difficult due to concerns about *face*, although this became less of an issue as relationships progressed and trust deepened.

As the experience of Will Percy indicates, it's vital that a coach is sensitive to cultural differences. This applies not only across nations, but also in different industries, professions or companies. I worked in a number of industrial companies for many years, and I've now been working in a university for 17 years. I find it very helpful to appreciate, for example, what is and isn't possible in the context of higher education. I'm not saying that one needs to have worked in a sector to be able to coach effectively in that area. But it's certainly essential to be open to appreciating the constraints and realities that your client faces in their particular setting.

In her book *The Culture Map*, Erin Meyer (2014) sets out a framework of eight dimensions along which national cultures vary. As an illustration of one dimension, in terms of communicating, some cultures (such as the USA or Britain) are *Low-Context*, which means that communication is precise, simple and clear. Other cultures (such as China or Japan) are *High-Context*, where communication is sophisticated, nuanced and layered. Meyer emphasises that it's the relative difference between two cultures that matters, not the absolute positions. If you are coaching someone from another country, or if you wish to explore how countries differ across the eight dimensions, you can purchase (fairly inexpensively) access to Meyer's Country Mapping Tool via this link: erinmeyer.com/tools/culture-map-premium/#price-table

Returning to my LeadershipPlus module, while I can appreciate how differences in cultural backgrounds are likely to influence our students, I cannot tailor my approach to each of the 120 or so individual students. What I can do, however, is to be sensitive to how students are responding. Similarly, if your work as a coach is with clients from different countries, it's vital to listen empathically and non-judgementally to understand as far as you can their reality. In his book *The Coaching Relationship in Practice*, Geoff Pelham acknowledges that a framework such as Meyer's is useful, but goes on to emphasise that:

> *Perhaps more fundamental, however, is a desire to reach out and 'meet' the other person, as underlying all the many differences there is a shared common humanity. In this sense working cross-culturally is not different to our usual practice, where the deepest challenge is always to connect with the other person.*

(Pelham, 2016)

One final point concerns your choice on how directive or non-directive you choose to be. Moving to the directive end of the spectrum, offering advice or suggestions based on your experience and worldview to someone whose cultural background and context is very different from your own, may well be inappropriate and unhelpful.

**VIDEO**

This four-minute video is an excellent summary of the eight dimensions of national culture in Erin Meyer's framework: www.youtube.com/watch?v=i92yIOSiBkc

## References

Meyer, E (2014) *The Culture Map: Decoding How People Think, Lead, and Get Things Done Across Cultures*. New York: PublicAffairs.

Pelham, G (2016) *The Coaching Relationship in Practice*. London: Sage.

# Chapter 4: D

## *DON'T JUST DO SOMETHING, SIT THERE*

In 2009 my first book on coaching, *Don't Just Do Something, Sit There*, was published. Its subtitle was *An Introduction to Non-directive Coaching*. Looking back at the book, I think the ideas that I shared there are still the basis of my practice, which I'd describe as a primarily non-directive approach to coaching.

I first heard the phrase that was the title of the book when I started a Certificate in Counselling at the University of Manchester in 1983. One of the tutors, George Henshaw, a wise and experienced counsellor who had set up the Manchester branch of the Samaritans, offered the words as a motto for the course. *'Don't just do something, sit there'* is a useful reminder if you want to engage in a conversation that's focused on the aims and needs of the other person.

My interest in taking the Certificate in Counselling came from my experience as a volunteer Samaritan, which I'd then been doing in the Warrington branch for a few years. I had found it rewarding to be able to listen to and support a caller who was in some form of distress. I wanted to deepen my understanding of how to engage in supportive conversations.

The implicit contract in a Samaritan call is that the caller can put the phone down at any time, and you probably never know what happens to them. I think that that experience helped me to learn to trust the client and their choices about what to do.

We'll touch on the importance of trust in coaching in a number of later chapters.

In that Certificate, we explored several approaches to counselling, including Carl Rogers' person-centred approach, Gestalt and cognitive-behavioural counselling. I still draw on ideas from these three perspectives, but it's the ideas of Carl Rogers that have had the most impact on my practice. Here are two vital ideas of Rogers that are foundations of a person-centred approach. (In their book *The Carl Rogers Reader*, Howard Kirschenbaum and Valerie Henderson offer an excellent overview of the ideas, writing and life of Carl Rogers.)

First, Rogers believes that each of us has an '*actualizing tendency*'. By this he means that each of us has within us the resources to understand ourself, to alter our sense of self and to modify our attitudes and behaviour. The person-centred approach is based on this fundamental trust in the client.

I think that the proposition that each of us has an actualising tendency is a big claim. However, in my practice, I'm prepared to accept it as a working hypothesis. In practical terms, this means that I trust the client to work out what's best for them and what they're prepared to do to pursue their goals or address their problems. It might take them time to work these out – not everything can be sorted within a coaching session. My experience as a Samaritan undoubtedly helps me to trust each of my coaching clients.

Second, in order to release the actualising tendency, Rogers states three core conditions that are both necessary and sufficient. If the client perceives that the counsellor or coach is offering a relationship based on: congruence (that is, the coach is being genuine); unconditional positive regard for the client (also described as non-judgemental acceptance); and empathic understanding, then the client is enabled to grow.

The combination of the two ideas is reflected in the metaphor that an acorn has all that is needed to become an oak tree, provided the right conditions of sunlight, water and nutrients are present.

Almost 40 years after taking the Certificate, my practice as a coach, supervisor and mediator is still hugely shaped by these ideas of Carl Rogers. My own definition of coaching today is essentially the same as the one I offered in *Don't Just Do Something, Sit There*. It is:

> *Coaching is a relationship of rapport and trust in which the coach uses their ability to listen, to ask questions and to play back what the client has communicated in order to help the client to clarify what matters to them and to work out what to do to achieve their aspirations.*

We'll unpick key terms in this definition in Chapter 8, '*How to Coach*'.

For a number of years I ran a Certificate in Coaching at the University of Warwick's Centre for Lifelong Learning. Having listened to me going on about the importance of a non-directive approach, one of the students gave me a wonderful piece of feedback. She said to me: '*You're very directive about being non-directive.*' Ouch! She was spot on. Since then, when I'm running sessions to help people learn how to coach, I take care to explain that, while my own approach to coaching is primarily non-directive, I'm not saying that this is the only, the best or the correct way to coach. Rather, I emphasise that I believe it's really important that a coach knows where they operate along the directive to non-directive spectrum. Understanding your own approach – both in an overall, philosophical sense and in the moment, when choosing what to say or do next within a coaching conversation – is an invaluable guide.

One of the other students on the Certificate shared with me his clear conclusion on this. He said something along these lines.

'*I work with unemployed young people in Coventry. They often have other problems, such as housing or drugs. I have 30-minute appointments. I have targets to get clients into work or training schemes. I can't be non-directive. I have to be directive.*' For me, that was a clear and appropriate statement of the basis of his practice.

Some years later I ran a couple of sessions on coaching with some people from China who were spending time studying at the Centre for Applied Linguistics at the University of Warwick. One of the students volunteered to be coached by me in a demonstration. To say thanks, I gave her a copy of *Don't Just Do Something, Sit There*. She shared the book around the group. After they returned to China, they arranged for it to be translated into Chinese. When the book was published in Chinese, the title when translated back to English was *Modern Midwifery: The Art of Coaching*. I wonder how it's catalogued!

According to Plato, Socrates used questions to help his students explore their ideas and come up with their own answers. His role was, like a midwife, to help people to give birth to their own ideas. Although I myself didn't use the term *Socratic questioning* in the text, the translator picked this as the key idea for the title in Chinese. We'll look at Socratic questioning again in the chapter on facilitation.

---

**REFLECTIVE TASK**

In my role as a senior tutor for half of the final year undergraduates at Warwick Business School, I draw on my coaching skills when meeting students. At times I move to the directive end of the spectrum – for instance, advising a student that they need formally to report mitigating circumstances that are affecting their ability to study and complete assessments.

Think of the various roles that you play.

- When do you believe it's important for you to be non-directive?
- And when is it more appropriate for you to be directive?

## References

Kirschenbaum, H and Henderson, V (eds) (1989) *The Carl Rogers Reader*. Boston: Houghton Mifflin.

Thomson, B (2009) *Don't Just Do Something, Sit There: An Introduction to Non-directive Coaching*. Oxford: Chandos Publishing.

# Chapter 5: E

## EMOTIONAL INTELLIGENCE

The term *emotional intelligence* (or EI) was popularised in the mid-1990s by Daniel Goleman, who wrote a book with this as its title. I think that the term, which he didn't invent, gave a form of legitimacy in the apparently rational and logical world of organisations to the importance of feelings and emotions in the workplace. I wouldn't want to overstate this, however. Many workplaces today are characterised by extreme focus on tasks at the expense of people.

The subtitle of Goleman's book is *Why It Can Matter More Than IQ*. He writes that, '*Emotional intelligence is twice as important as cognitive abilities in predicting employee performance and accounts for more than 85% of star performance in top leaders*' (Goleman, 1996). I don't know how accurate these claims are, but they suggest that possessing emotional intelligence is an invaluable asset for staff, managers and leaders. Goleman also suggests that, in contrast to IQ which is more or less fixed, you can learn how to become more emotionally intelligent. Practice, feedback and coaching are some ways to do this.

In the opening pages Goleman quotes the ancient Greek philosopher Aristotle:

> *Anyone can become angry – that is easy. But to be angry with the right person, to the right degree, at the right time, for the right purpose, and in the right way – that is not easy.*
>
> (quoted in Goleman, 1996)

I'm not sure I agree with Aristotle here. I think that some people find it very difficult to be angry – or perhaps, more exactly, to acknowledge or to show that they're feeling angry.

However, the quote illustrates the importance of both being aware of how we feel and then knowing how to respond appropriately. Figure 5.1 summarises neatly four key aspects of emotional intelligence. (Goleman includes a fifth characteristic, *Motivation*, in his framework.)

**Figure 5.1  A framework for emotional intelligence**

|  | SELF | OTHERS |
|---|---|---|
| RESPONSIBILITY | *Self-management* | *Social skills* |
| AWARENESS | *Self-awareness* | *Empathy* |

EI starts with *self-awareness*, the ability to recognise what you're feeling at a point in time. It can be helpful to be able to put a name to the emotion you're experiencing. A simple exercise is to add just one word to complete the sentence '*I feel ...*'. I've found that when I ask someone how they feel, more often than not they tell me what they think. If you can insert the word '*that*' to '*I feel ...*' without changing the meaning, then what follows almost certainly is a thought rather than a feeling. (For example, '*I feel [that] this was an interesting sentence*'.)

The other aspect of awareness is awareness of the other person – noticing what's going on for them. This may be termed *empathy*.

Note that empathy is different from sympathy. Sympathy is about imagining how you would feel if you were in the other person's situation. Empathy is about understanding how they are feeling in their situation.

In the opening chapter we looked at the equation which captures the essence of good coaching:

Awareness + responsibility = performance

Let's move on from awareness – of yourself and of others – to responsibility. What do you do with your awareness? Someone who is emotionally intelligent is able to manage how they respond in the light of the emotion that they're feeling.

As an illustration, let's return to the quote from Aristotle and imagine that you're feeling angry. *Self-management* is about what you do with this feeling. In some situations – maybe a meeting in the workplace – it might be disastrous to show or talk about your anger. In other situations – perhaps in a courageous conversation – it could be valuable to share that you're feeling angry. To be angry in the right way isn't easy!

Similarly, as you become aware of how the other person is feeling, you need to choose how to respond. An emotionally intelligent person has a range of *social skills* that enable them to respond appropriately and effectively to a wide range of people and situations. This is vital in managing people well.

Emotional intelligence is also important for a coach. By their very nature, coaching conversations often involve deep feelings about things that matter to a client. And the coach may well have their own emotional reaction to what the client is conveying. In a coaching relationship, having an empathic understanding of the client – their hopes and fears, their values and constraints, and so on – is essential. Listening to understand the client and their world is the foundation for this. And the questions you ask, the ideas you share, the exercises you propose are based on this understanding.

In the moment within a session, what you do in response to the client is always a judgement. You might choose to play back to the client your appreciation of their situation, which can help to build rapport and trust in the relationship. There might also be times when simply sitting with the silence demonstrates respect and concern for what the client is thinking or feeling. Inviting the client to explore in more detail or depth important feelings might or might not be appropriate.

Not only is it important to empathically understand the client, it's also essential to convey this to the client so that they feel understood and accepted without judgement by the coach. This helps to build a relationship of rapport and trust. I love this quote from Meg Wheatley's book *Turning to One Another*:

> *Why is being heard so healing? I don't know the full answer to that question, but I do know that it has something to do with the fact that listening creates relationship.*
>
> (Wheatley, 2002)

In closing this chapter, let me emphasise the importance of how, as a coach, you need to be aware of and to manage your emotional responses to a client. This might be termed *use of self*. Michael Frisch offers this working definition:

> *Use of self: A coach's thought or feeling reaction to a client that the coach is both aware of and will use, either directly or indirectly, in the service of the coaching.*
>
> (Frisch, 2008, p 12)

We explore this topic in Chapter 32, 'Use of self' when we look at how, as a coach, you might use what is going on within you in a conversation. Once again, the coach is continually making judgements about what, if anything, to share of their reactions to a client – and how to do this. The emotionally intelligent use of oneself is an advanced coaching skill.

**VIDEO**

In this three-minute animated video Brené Brown brilliantly explores empathy and how it differs from sympathy: www.youtube.com/watch?v=1Evwgu369Jw

## References

Frisch, M (2008) *Use of Self in Executive Coaching.* New York: i-Coach Coaching Monograph Series. [online] Available at: https://icoachnewyork.com/wp-content/uploads/2015/09/Monograph.pdf (accessed 24 August 2022).

Goleman, D (1996) *Emotional Intelligence: Why It Can Matter More Than IQ.* London: Bloomsbury.

Wheatley, M (2002) *Turning to One Another: Simple Conversations to Restore Hope to the Future.* San Francisco: Berrett-Koehler.

# Chapter 6: F

## FEEDBACK

Feedback is an important aspect of coaching. A coaching relationship, particularly one where trust and rapport have been established, offers a special opportunity for feedback. In offering feedback to a coaching client, it's useful to be clear about your intent – *why am I giving this feedback to this client now?* It's also important to choose your words carefully to maximise the likelihood that the client will both understand and consider your feedback.

I think that feedback needs to be specific. As an illustration, imagine that I've just delivered a PowerPoint presentation, and received these three pieces of feedback.

1. I really liked your slides.
2. I didn't think your slides were very good.
3. The font on your slides was small, which meant that the people at the back of the room couldn't read the text.

Only the third statement is useful. It's specific, it describes the impact, and I can do something to improve for next time.

*Giving* feedback – saying what you think went well and what didn't go well, or telling how it could have been done better – is moving towards the directive end of the spectrum. This may be entirely appropriate and helpful. An alternative is to *generate* feedback by first asking the individual to reflect upon and assess their own performance. For example, imagine that you are a line manager and one of your staff has produced a report. To invite them to generate their own feedback, you can simply ask them some open questions, such as the following.

- What were you pleased about in your report?
- What were you less pleased about?
- What did you learn about how to write a report?
- What will you do differently next time?
- Any other reflections?

The individual might cover everything that you would have said, but they are likely to have more sense of ownership and more commitment to doing things better next time than if you'd simply told them what you thought was good and less good. And, if they miss something important, you can add this after they've finished their reflection. This combination of asking and, if necessary, telling is more likely to raise awareness and encourage responsibility.

It can be useful as part of the contracting at the start of a coaching relationship to clarify with the client what they expect in the way of feedback from you and what you agree to offer. Agreeing, for example, that you will at times move to the directive end of the spectrum and give feedback might be what the client wants and perhaps needs. Nevertheless, in my own practice, I generally invite the client to explore their thinking first before I offer my views.

A different but related point is *reality checking*. For example, a client may be settling on an action plan for which I have some reservations. I then have a decision on whether and how to invite them to check how realistic their plans are. I also have a choice on the form of words that I use. On the one hand, I might make a statement beginning with something like '*I have some reservations about your plan …*'. Or, I might ask a question such as '*What are the risks if you carry out your plan?*' One thing

I avoid is asking a leading question, one that contains a suggested answer, such as *'Is there a risk that your plan will damage the relationship with your colleague?'* In this example, I prefer to make a statement such as, *'I'm concerned about the impact your plan will have on the relationship with your colleague.'*

Another aspect of feedback that is usefully addressed in contracting is when there is a three-way contract between an organisation (perhaps represented by a boss or an HR business partner), a client (the person being coached) and a coach. Some coaches are happy to give feedback on the client to the organisation, and sometimes this is a key reason why the coaching is being proposed in the first place. And other coaches will simply refuse to give feedback, regarding this as compromising confidentiality and limiting the development of trust in the relationship. Again, clarity on what, if anything, will be fed back to the organisation is a vital part of contracting.

One form of feedback that is sometimes part of a coaching assignment is 360-degree feedback. This is generally gathered via a questionnaire completed by people around the client – such as their manager, their colleagues, the people that they manage, their clients and themselves. A report is generated, and the coach takes the client through this. I notice that often the client finds the responses given to open-ended questions more useful than ratings based, for instance, on replies to statements on a *Strongly disagree* to *Strongly agree* Likert scale. I once spoke to a former client who still remembered vividly what their boss had written in a 360-degree feedback exercise ten years previously. We'll look at 360-degree feedback again in the chapter on 'Psychometric instruments and 360-degree feedback'.

A different issue is how you as a coach gather feedback on your practice. It can be useful from time to time to ask the client for feedback on their experience of being coached by you. You might use questions such as:

- What do I do that is particularly helpful?
- What do I do that isn't helpful?
- What would you like me to do more of? Less of?
- What needs to shift in our relationship as coach and client?

Asking questions such as these can be helpful halfway through an assignment, allowing changes to be made for the remaining sessions. Or they might be asked at the end of an assignment, providing ideas to consider for future relationships with other clients. It can be useful to share the feedback in supervision too, allowing you to explore more deeply your strengths and weaknesses as a coach.

**REFLECTIVE TASK**

Think about a piece of work – perhaps a coaching conversation or relationship – that you have carried out recently. Here are some questions to generate some feedback for yourself.

- What do you think you did well?
- What might you have done better?
- What did you do that you're unsure of?
- What lessons will you draw from these reflections to take into future work?

# Chapter 7: G

## THE GROW MODEL

In Britain the GROW model is probably the best-known framework for structuring a coaching conversation. Developed originally by Graham Alexander, it was popularised by John Whitmore in his book *Coaching for Performance*. The mnemonic is based on these four elements:

**G**oal        What are you trying to achieve?

**R**eality        What is currently going on?

**O**ptions        What might you do?

**W**ill        What will you do?

When I'm running an introductory coaching skills workshop or programme, I use an exercise called *silent coaching* to explain the model. I invite each participant to identify an issue they're currently facing. The issue needs to be real, to matter to them, to be one where they personally are involved and where they're not sure what to do. I explain that I'll pose 20 questions for them to answer in writing. I assure them that I don't expect them to share anything with anyone else, so their reflections can be as deep or personal as they wish. I ask them to write down in one sentence what the issue is. I then go through these questions:

Goal

1. What are you trying to achieve?
2. Imagine that you have successfully addressed your issue. What does success look like?

3. And what does success feel like?
4. In regard to this issue, what do you really, really want?

Reality

5. What is happening that makes this an issue for you?
6. What are the key features of the situation?
7. Who is involved?
8. What assumptions are you making?
9. What – if anything – have you already done to address the situation?
10. And what has been the effect of what you have done so far?

Options

11. What options do you have?
12. What else might you do?
13. If you had absolutely no constraints – of time or money or power or health – what would you do?
14. If you had a really wise friend, what would they do in your shoes?

Will

15. Your answers to the last four questions have generated a set of options. Which options will you actually pursue?
16. For each chosen option, what specifically will you do?
17. What help or support do you need?
18. What deadlines will you set for yourself?
19. What is the first step that you will take?

I finish with a final question which is about the process rather than the content of their reflections, noting that I'd like to hear from some of them how they answered this.

20. What was the effect of these questions?

The exercise is usually very useful in helping many of the participants to become clearer about their issue or about what they can do to tackle it. The structured questions help to raise awareness and/or to encourage responsibility. And, for a few participants, it doesn't make much difference. I suspect that this is likely to have something to do with the nature of the issue they chose.

As well as introducing the GROW model, the exercise demonstrates the power of being non-directive (I don't even know what the issues are), and of asking short, open questions. When I later invite the participants to coach one another in pairs or trios, they often use the questions somewhat mechanically. My hope is that, with further practice, they realise that their questions need to emerge from listening to understand the client. There is nothing magical about these particular questions.

Questions like those in the silent coaching exercise can be useful to do some *self-coaching* in order to work systematically through a problem, challenge or opportunity by writing down your answers. You might like to try this out.

It's important to use the GROW framework flexibly. Sometimes the client is very clear about their Goal, but the current Reality is complex and confusing. Sometimes we get to Options and the client realises that there isn't anything practical that can be done to achieve the Goal – we might then go back to modify or perhaps even abandon the Goal. Sometimes the client recognises that the real issue is different to what we've been exploring. All of these might be valuable insights. The world's problems don't all fall neatly into 20-minute challenges.

I myself have the framework at the back of my mind when I'm coaching. I don't often explicitly go through the four stages, but sometimes I recognise that, for example, it seems appropriate to explore Options or to invite the client to be more specific about what they Will do.

One thing that I generally do is to ask two other questions near the start of a coaching conversation. I'll ask something like, '*What do you want to talk about today?*' This establishes a *Topic* for the session. I'll then ask something along the lines of, '*What would be a useful outcome for you from our conversation today?*' This establishes a more focused *Objective* for the conversation. We might then go on to use the GROW model for the remainder of the conversation. So we could expand the GROW model to become the TO GROW model:

| | |
|---|---|
| **T**opic | What do you want to talk about today? |
| **O**bjective | What would be a useful outcome from this conversation? |
| **G**oal | What are you trying to achieve? |
| **R**eality | What is currently going on? |
| **O**ptions | What could you do? |
| **W**ill | What will you do? |

John Whitmore recommends exploring Goal before Reality as he reckons that this will produce a more creative and motivating action plan. However, I find that it's often more natural to begin by exploring the current Reality before moving on to the client's Goal. But RGOW isn't as memorable at GROW!

You can use the GROW framework in working with a team rather than an individual. Agreeing a shared Goal may be more challenging with a team, and there will inevitably be different perspectives on the current Reality. It might also be harder to reach agreement on and commitment to an action plan. The one element where a team may find it easier than an individual is in generating a range of Options.

I find that participants on a coaching skills programme are often able to recall later the GROW model. But it's just one way of structuring a conversation. A much more fundamental idea in coaching is the importance of raising Awareness and encouraging Responsibility.

**VIDEO**

In this seven-minute video Dee Wilkinson from South West Coaching takes a fictitious client through a conversation based on the four steps in the GROW model: www.youtube.com/watch?v=6f3X2PEsV-Q

## Reference

Whitmore, J (2002) *Coaching for Performance: The Principles of Coaching and Leadership*. London: Nicholas Brealey.

# Chapter 8: H

## *HOW TO COACH*

In 2014, Sage published my book *First Steps in Coaching*. I agreed to write a second edition, which they published in 2020. Much of the content was the same, but there was fresh material and the new text was one-third longer. Someone at Sage proposed that the second edition have the title *How to Coach*. I really liked the title, although I had some concerns that it might give the impression that the book is more of a definitive statement than I intended. It sounds too directive for my taste! We also agreed the subtitle, which reflected the title of the first edition, *First Steps and Beyond*.

In *How to Coach* I use the same definition of coaching that I'm using in this book:

> *Coaching is a relationship of rapport and trust in which the coach uses their ability to listen, to ask questions and to play back what the client has communicated in order to help the client to clarify what matters to them and to work out what to do to achieve their aspirations.*
>
> (Thomson, 2020)

Let's unpick the definition to explore what it suggests about how to coach.

It begins '*Coaching is a relationship ...*'. This isn't grammatically correct. Coaching is a process, rather than a relationship. But I think that the relationship between coach and client is so fundamentally important that I begin my definition with this phrase.

In his book *Relational Coaching*, published in 2008, Erik de Haan explores the question *'How does coaching work?'* He suggests that at that time there hadn't been enough research done to answer the question clearly. However, there had been plenty of reputable research carried out into how psychotherapy and counselling work. These professions were established well before coaching began to become popular. He carries out a meta-analysis of this research, and concludes that the most important factors affecting the outcome of therapy are:

- the quality of the relationship;
- the person of the therapist;
- the client – probably the most important factor in therapy; and
- the support, trials and tribulations experienced by the client outside the therapy.

He suggests that it's likely that these findings will also apply to coaching – which, he recognises, is something of a leap. He goes on to say:

> *My view of coaching now is that coaching is predominantly an exercise in* self-understanding *and* self-changing *on the part of the coachee.*
>
> *Coachees do the actual work all by themselves, and the only thing that coaching can do is to help them find and activate their natural, inherent abilities.*
>
> *The only thing the coach can actually influence … is the* relationship *between coach and coachee.*
>
> (de Haan, 2008, emphasis in original)

My definition proposes two terms to characterise the nature of an effective coaching relationship – rapport and trust. Both may take time to develop. And both go two ways. I think this is obvious in terms of rapport. But it's also true of trust. The client trusts the coach, appreciating that they are in their corner, supporting their best interests. And the coach trusts the client, allowing them the freedom to make their own decisions and choices.

The definition then states the three key conversational skills needed to coach well – listening to understand the client, asking mainly short, open questions, and playing back to the client what they've said or perhaps communicated non-verbally. We look at these skills in three later chapters. I think that listening is the fundamental skill that the coach needs – the ability to listen non-judgementally and empathically to understand the client and their world. Asking mainly short, open questions that follow the interest of the client and help them to explore their world follows from having first listened. And playing back an empathic and reasonably accurate appreciation to the client can show them that they've been heard, understood and accepted. And this helps to establish rapport and trust.

The final two clauses are what makes this a definition of primarily non-directive coaching. Coaching is about helping the client to clarify what they're seeking and to make plans to achieve their ambitions. My view is that coaching is about facilitating, not instructing, advising or guiding. Of course, one can do these things and one can call them coaching, but it's not what I mean by coaching. Indeed, if you asked the ordinary person in the street what they thought coaching was, many will reply with an example such as a soccer coach. People such as Jürgen Klopp and Pep Guardiola are coaches – and they are paid vastly more than I am. As a lifetime football fan, I really admire what they do. But I imagine that their definition of coaching will be different from mine.

In his book, Erik de Haan proposes ten commandments for an executive coach that were suggested by his review of how therapy works (de Haan, 2008). This prompted me to offer my own ten commandments for a coach. I'm conscious of the irony in offering commandments on how to coach non-directively! I invite you to treat these as prompts for reflection rather than commandments. I'm also once again reminded of the brilliant piece of feedback that I once received which I mentioned in the chapter *Don't Just Do Something, Sit There*: '*You're very directive about being non-directive!*'

Anyway, here are my ten commandments – or prompts for reflection – on how to coach.

1. Listen non-judgementally to understand the client.
2. Ask crisp, open questions to help the client explore their situation, their goals and their action plans.
3. Play back with empathy your understanding to the client.
4. Trust the client.
5. Trust yourself, your experience and your intuition.
6. Trust the coaching process.
7. Reflect on your practice, including with an experienced supervisor.
8. Recognise when there's some interference getting in the way of you coaching fluently – and put it out of your mind.
9. Explore what tools you wish to use within your coaching practice.
10. Behave ethically.

We'll discuss ideas such as supervision, interference, tools and ethics in later chapters.

**READING**

The link below is an article by Erik de Haan where he sets out his ten commandments for an executive coach, based on his review of research into how psychotherapy works: www.erikdehaan.com/wp-content/uploads/2013/09/2007 _TJ_Ten-commandments.pdf

## References

de Haan, E (2008) *Relational Coaching: Journeys Towards Mastering One-to-One Learning*. Chichester: John Wiley.

Thomson, B (2014) *First Steps in Coaching*. London: Sage.

Thomson, B (2020) *How to Coach: First Steps and Beyond*. London: Sage.

# Chapter 9: I

## INNER GAME OF COACHING

Timothy Gallwey was an American educationalist whose book, *The Inner Game of Tennis*, first published in 1974, has been hugely influential in shaping a primarily non-directive approach to coaching. John Whitmore and Myles Downey, who were leaders as coaching developed in Britain, studied and worked with Gallwey. I myself first learnt about coaching by attending a course run by Myles, and I later worked with John and his colleagues to run coaching skills programmes for managers at the gas pipeline company Transco. Hence, my own approach which I'm sharing in this book owes much to Gallwey's ideas.

Gallwey had been a talented tennis player in his youth. He recalls an incident when he froze at match point in a national tournament, mis-hitting what would have been an easy winner. It wasn't lack of tennis skill that caused this, but rather what was going on inside his head. The *outer game* of tennis is played against an opponent on the other side of the net. The *inner game* of tennis, Gallwey wrote, is:

> the game that takes place in the mind of the player, and it is played against such obstacles as lapses in concentration, nervousness, self-doubt and self-condemnation. In short, it is played to overcome all habits of mind which inhibit excellence in performance.
>
> (Gallwey, 1974)

Gallwey hypothesised that within each of us is a *Self One* and a *Self Two*. Self One is a conscious self who does not trust Self Two and continually tells Self Two what to do through various commands and injunctions, many of which are critical and unhelpful. Self Two is an unconscious automatic self who can perform lots of things gracefully and fluently. In his book *Effective Coaching*, Myles Downey writes that Self One is characterised by tension, fear, doubt and trying too hard, whereas Self Two is characterised by relaxed concentration, enjoyment and trust.

The undermining chatter of our Self One – *your backhand is rubbish, you'll never control this volley, that winner must have been a fluke* – is *interference*. It gets in the way of our performing to our potential. Gallwey summarised this in an equation:

$$Performance = potential - interference$$

Let's look at how these ideas can affect your ability to coach fluently and well. I sometimes notice, generally about ten minutes into a coaching conversation, that I'm saying to myself something along the lines of *'Oh dear, this is a real mess, how am I going to get them out of this?'* This thinking is interference. It's not my job to solve the client's problem – rather, my job is to manage the session to help them explore and, perhaps, solve their problem. There's a great quote from Myles Downey which captures this brilliantly:

> *The primary function of the coach is to understand, not to solve, fix, heal, make better or be wise – to understand. The magic is that it is in that moment of understanding that the coachees themselves understand for themselves, become more aware and are then in a position to make better decisions and choices than they would have done*

*anyway. That is how coaching is profoundly simple and simply profound. But most of us struggle to get above our own agenda and want to be seen to be making a difference.*

(Downey, 2003)

Another interference that I often notice in people at the early stages of learning how to coach is that they feel the need to do a great job for their coachee. This might take the form of thinking that they have to ask a brilliant question. They stop listening to understand, and instead focus on wording their next question. Of course, one wants to ask good and helpful questions. But, if we think too hard about this, it gets in the way of coaching well. Paradoxically, trying too hard to do a good job gets in the way of actually doing a good job.

In their book *Coaching, Mentoring and Organizational Consultancy*, Peter Hawkins and Nick Smith write about an interference that can affect even very experienced coaches from time to time which they call the *'deference threshold'*. This occurs when *'it feels that the client or the situation have rendered us considerably less effective than we normally are'* (Hawkins and Smith, 2006). This might be an unconscious reaction to the client. The coach *'defers'* to the client, becomes ineffective, or feels a need for the approval of the client.

One way of managing these interferences lies in two steps which are easy to state but may be harder to implement. First, simply notice the interference. You might call this being mindful of what's happening within yourself. Second, put the thought to one side and bring your attention back fully to coaching your client.

Another idea which I find very helpful in managing interference during a coaching session is about trust. As we noted in the previous chapter, as a coach I need to:

- trust the client to know what's right for them;
- trust myself to draw on my experience and intuition;
- trust the coaching process.

If I can, in Downey's words, let go of the need *'to solve, fix, heal, make better or be wise'* (Downey, 2003), but instead pay great attention to the client and what is unfolding in the conversation, then I'm much more likely to coach effectively.

Coaching often, but not always, works. In a later book, *The Inner Game of Work*, Gallwey writes:

> *Coaching cannot be done in a vacuum. If the learner doesn't want to learn, it doesn't make any difference if the coach is a great coach. Coaching is a dance in which the learner, not the coach, is the leader.*

(Gallwey, 2000)

I find this reassuring. I hope that my coaching is valuable for my clients. But if my Self One is telling me that every session I have has to be successful, this is likely to be an interference that gets in the way of my coaching fluently.

---

**REFLECTIVE TASK**

As Myles Downey notes, tension, fear, doubt and trying too hard are interferences that are likely to get in the way of us performing well. The term *self-talk* refers to the things that we say to ourselves – inside our head, as it were. Self-talk can be positive and helpful, or negative and unhelpful.

Think about an activity that you engage in. It could be coaching, or something connected to work, or something else, such as a leisure activity.

- What unhelpful, unspoken messages do you sometimes tell yourself about how you perform in this activity?
- What might be more helpful but still realistic messages to tell yourself?

## References

Downey, M (2003) *Effective Coaching: Lessons from the Coach's Coach*. London: Texere.

Gallwey, W T (1974) *The Inner Game of Tennis*. London: Jonathan Cape.

Gallwey, W T (2000) *The Inner Game of Work: Overcoming Mental Obstacles for Maximum Performance*. New York: Random House.

Hawkins, P and Smith, N (2006) *Coaching, Mentoring and Organizational Consultancy: Supervision, Skills and Development*. Maidenhead: Open University Press.

# Chapter 10: J

## JUDGEMENT

In a coaching conversation, you are continually making judgements about what to say or do next. We explore this in the first half of this chapter. And, in order to create a deep relationship of trust and rapport, you need to accept non-judgementally the client as a person, as a unique and valuable human being. We discuss this in the second half of the chapter. So, making judgements sits alongside being non-judgemental!

Coaching is an art rather than a science. While a coach might, for example, use the GROW framework to structure a conversation, they cannot simply work mechanically through a predetermined set of questions. Good coaching questions emerge from listening attentively to understand the client. The coach frequently has to make choices in the moment on how they will respond to what a client is saying or perhaps communicating non-verbally. *Do I ask a question, or offer a playback? Do I suggest an exercise at this point? Do I let a silence run or not?* And then, *what specifically will I say?*

The judgements that you make as a coach about what to say or do next not only structure the conversation but also shape your relationship with the client. A point that I emphasise in many places in this book is that it's vital as a coach that you are clear where you operate on the directive to non-directive spectrum – and why. If you operate frequently from the directive end of the spectrum, offering advice or suggestions, you will create a very different relationship than if you work primarily from the non-directive end. Both approaches might be effective, and this will depend on factors such as the context, the particular client and the nature of the issue.

In making judgements in the moment within a session, a coach is likely to draw upon their experience and their intuition. There is an analogy with a game of chess. One move may set up a particular game, while another move sets up a different one. You won't know what would have happened if you'd played the move that you didn't choose. Similarly, a particular question or exercise may take a coaching conversation in one direction. You may not know what would have happened if you'd made a different choice. (All metaphors are partial, and hence limited. While you can't go back in a chess match and change your move, you might be able to ask that coaching question later. Another difference is that chess is a contest where both players are trying to win. Coaching isn't a competition!)

It's helpful not to overthink this. In his book *Effective Coaching*, Myles Downey offers this reassuring thought:

> *Coaching is not an exam where you get only one chance. If a question does not work, ask another. When you are in a good relationship it does not matter. There is only one mistake that you can make in coaching and that is to irreparably damage the relationship.*
>
> (Downey, 2003)

Drawing on your intuition in the moment to judge what to say next is an example of how as a coach you make use of yourself. We discuss this in a later chapter, 'Use of self'. Developing trust in yourself, and avoiding interferences such as *I must ask a great question* or *I have to add value*, is an important part of your journey of development as a coach.

Let's turn now to the importance of non-judgementally accepting the client. The views and philosophy of Carl Rogers are one of the key foundations of my approach to coaching. Non-judgemental acceptance – which he also calls unconditional positive regard – is one of Rogers' three core conditions that create the necessary and sufficient conditions for the client to draw upon their self-actualising tendency in order to grow, develop and realise their potential. (The other two conditions are communicating empathic understanding, and being congruent or genuine in the relationship.) Rogers writes:

> *Acceptance involves the therapist's willingness for the client to be whatever immediate feeling is going on – confusion, resentment, fear, anger, courage, love, or pride. It is a nonpossessive caring. When the therapist prizes the client in a total rather than a conditional way, forward movement is likely.*
>
> (quoted in Kirschenbaum and Henderson, 1989)

Similarly, in a coaching context, I believe it's vital that I accept each client unconditionally and non-judgementally as a unique and valuable human being. I may have a view that some of their actions are unwise or selfish or uncaring, but I need to accept them non-judgementally as a person. In his early writings Rogers described his approach as *non-directive*, but changed the term to *person-centred*. In describing how I coach, I say that I am primarily non-directive, but it might be appropriate to call it client-centred coaching. (This raises a different question as to who is the client – the person sat opposite me or the organisation which is paying for the coaching. We touched on the issue of three-way contracting in Chapter 6, 'Feedback'.)

You may find it interesting to reflect upon the people that you find it easy to accept non-judgementally and those that you find it difficult or perhaps even impossible to accept non-judgementally. Many years ago I attended a workshop on Dialogue facilitated by Peter Garrett. One of the things that Peter did was to go into prisons and facilitate conversations with people who had committed crimes such as murder, rape or child sex abuse. My impression was that he could unconditionally accept these people. I've never attempted it, but I don't think I could do this work.

One final thought on being non-judgemental is in relation to working with clients from different cultures. As an illustration, in my role as an academic at Warwick Business School I sometimes teach groups that include a significant number of students from China. The culture and educational system in China are both very different from those in Britain. Students are not accustomed to an approach where they are expected to contribute actively to class discussions. They are also speaking in a second language. Not only do I need to make practical allowances for such factors, but I also must avoid making a judgement that someone from another culture who isn't contributing to a group discussion is somehow less capable or intelligent.

**VIDEO**

In this short video (under two minutes), Carl Rogers reflects upon a conversation where he had to strive to unconditionally and empathically accept a client: www.youtube.com/watch?v=o0neRQzudzw

## References

Downey, M (2003) *Effective Coaching: Lessons from the Coach's Coach.* London: Texere.

Kirschenbaum, H and Henderson, V (eds) (1989) *The Carl Rogers Reader.* Boston: Houghton Mifflin.

# Chapter 11: K

## KOLB LEARNING CYCLE

I started working in management development in 1988 when I joined the British Gas Management Centre near Stratford upon Avon. It was based in a lovely country house that was later converted into homes and flats after British Gas split itself in two in the mid-1990s. For more than 30 years, David Kolb's cycle of learning from experience has been the foundation of my practice as a facilitator of learning and development.

In his book *The Fifth Discipline*, Peter Senge (1990) writes about *real learning*, which he defines as becoming *'able to do something we never were able to do'*. Deep and sustained learning – becoming able to do something you couldn't do before – only comes through experience. However, experience on its own isn't enough. In order to learn, you need to reflect upon and make sense of your experience. And your learning and capability deepen when you try to do things differently as a result of your sense making.

In his book *Experiential Learning*, David Kolb (1984) describes this process as a learning cycle. Figure 11.1 shows a diagram of the experiential learning cycle, in my words rather than Kolb's.

The cycle is also captured in Kolb's definition of learning as *'the process whereby knowledge is created through the transformation of experience'* (Kolb, 1984). You go around the learning cycle to transform your experience into knowledge.

**Figure 11.1 The cycle of learning from experience**

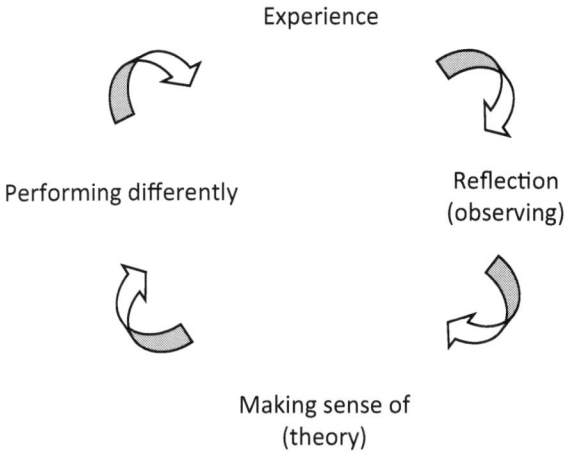

Experience

Performing differently

Reflection
(observing)

Making sense of
(theory)

It's possible to start the cycle at any point. For example, reading these words about a theory of learning might prompt you to try out a new approach in your teaching. Or, observing how someone chairs a meeting well (or indeed badly) might give you pointers (in this context, another word for *theory*) on how you will chair your own meetings.

As a management development professional and as a professor at Warwick Business School, I regard my role not as a teacher but rather as a facilitator of learning. This isn't just semantics – it has important implications for what I do. Whenever I'm designing a learning event – which might range from a 20-minute exercise to a one-day workshop to a five-week leadership programme – I seek to create opportunities for each participant to:

- have an experience;
- reflect on this, or on previous experiences;
- consider ideas, models and theories;
- try things out, either during the event or afterwards.

In his book *On Becoming a Person*, Carl Rogers (1961) wrote some words that have also influenced my approach and which are a challenge to anyone who teaches: '*It seems to me that anything that can be taught to another is relatively inconsequential, and has little or no influence on behavior.*' This echoes some words of Galileo that are very relevant to a non-directive approach to coaching: '*You cannot teach people anything. You can only help them to discover it within themselves.*'

Let me illustrate how I draw upon the four elements of the experiential learning cycle in a programme that I run at the University of Warwick. It is an optional, not-for-credit Certificate in Coaching Practice taken by some second-year undergraduates. It is based on five two-hour sessions, one per fortnight. The sessions involve a mix of input from me or through short videos, exercises to introduce tools such as the GROW model, rich pictures or reflective writing, questions for reflection, and discussion.

There are two activities aimed at giving the students an opportunity to practise and develop their coaching skills. First, within several sessions, the students coach each other in groups of three. In their group, each student has a short opportunity to coach a colleague, to be coached and to observe a coaching conversation. Second, the students are asked to find a practice client, someone who is willing to have three coaching sessions with them over a few weeks or months. This gives them the opportunity not only to practise conversational skills but also to think about practical aspects such as keeping notes, finding a suitable venue and reviewing actions agreed at the previous session. The certificate is assessed rather lightly through a 1,000-word reflective essay where each student addresses these three questions:

1. What are the advantages and disadvantages in coaching from the non-directive end of the spectrum?

2.  Critically appraise your listening and questioning skills.
3.  Identify three key insights that you took from the certificate that you will use in future conversations.

In such a short programme, I do not make any attempt to assess the quality of each student's coaching skills. One piece of learning that most of the participants take from their experience is the insight that they don't have to offer advice or suggestions whenever a friend or colleague asks for help.

One way of reflecting upon and making sense of experience is the idea of journaling. A journal isn't a diary; rather, it's a place to record and reflect upon important experiences. For example, a coach might ask a client who is finding it difficult to speak up in certain meetings to write afterwards about how they thought, felt or behaved during these meetings. They might then discuss this together in the next coaching session. Over time, the client may become aware of triggers or patterns of behaviour – and might then make changes in how they think and behave. In their book *Reflective Writing in Counselling and Psychotherapy*, Jeannie Wright and Gillie Bolton (2012) say that: *'Journal writing has the power to help people understand themselves, each other, their relationships with each other and their world better.'* And, of course, you as a coach might keep a journal to reflect upon your own practice. Looking back at what you wrote some time ago, you might see how your practice has evolved – or perhaps stagnated. We'll look at journaling again in Chapter 23, 'Writing'.

In another chapter we'll look at supervision of coaching. Supervision provides a space for a coach to reflect in depth on their experiences in their coaching practice. This can enable them to develop their skills and confidence as a coach. It is also an opportunity to consider what they might do differently, either with a particular client or more generally in their practice. And the supervisor might offer an idea, model or tool that the coach can consider using. In other words, there is an opportunity in coaching supervision for the supervisee to visit each of the four points on the experiential learning cycle.

**VIDEO**

It's possible to move all around the learning cycle in a few minutes – or you can be stuck without progressing for years. This short, animated video describes well the experiential learning cycle and includes some additional points on how to learn effectively: www.youtube.com/watch?v=46Uk XjbAqG8

## References

Kolb, D (1984) *Experiential Learning: Experience as the Source of Learning and Development*. Englewood Cliffs: Prentice-Hall.

Rogers, C (1961) *On Becoming a Person: A Therapist's View of Psychotherapy*. Boston: Houghton Mifflin.

Senge, P (1990) *The Fifth Discipline: The Art and Practice of the Learning Organization*. New York: Currency Doubleday.

Wright, J and Bolton, G (2012) *Reflective Writing in Counselling and Psychotherapy.* London: Sage.

# Chapter 12: L

## LISTENING

Listening is the fundamental skill in coaching. The questions you ask, the playbacks you offer, the exercises you introduce and the ideas and models you share all flow from listening to understand the client and their world. Moreover, demonstrating to the client that you've listened with empathy and acceptance to them helps to build the relationship between you – and coaching is essentially a relationship of rapport and trust.

In coaching workshops I often introduce the idea of a ladder of listening, illustrated in Figure 12.1. The bottom rung is 'Not listening'. In my experience of working in organisations, this is the most common form of listening.

**Figure 12.1 The ladder of listening**

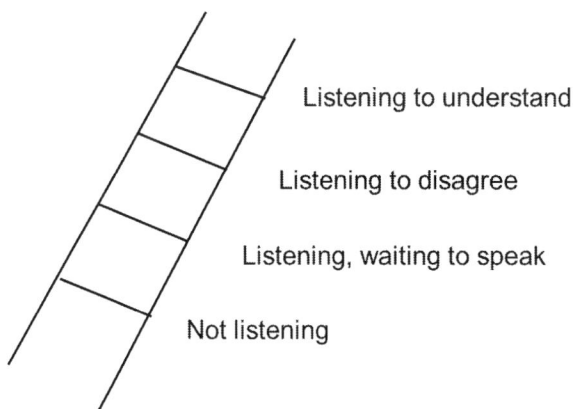

Listening to understand

Listening to disagree

Listening, waiting to speak

Not listening

The next rung up is 'Listening, waiting to speak'. This is when your focus is on what you're going to say when the other person stops talking. In a coaching conversation, this often manifests itself as the coach focusing on the next question they're going to ask. This is also known as 'Listening to respond'. The danger in this is that you stop listening to what the client is saying as you think about your question. It's better to wait until the client has finished speaking and then, if necessary, take a few moments to decide what you'll say or do next.

Further up is 'Listening to disagree'. This is typical of what goes on in many meetings. I have a point of view, and you have a different point of view. I want to show that my view is better. I may want the meeting to agree to my idea. So, I'll listen selectively to what you say, looking out for any weaknesses, which I'll then pounce on. It's about winning and losing. I will attack your position, and defend my own. If you're ever charged with murder, this is the quality of listening that you want your barrister to be good at. But it's not helpful in a coaching conversation.

The top rung of the ladder – 'Listening to understand' – is the type of listening needed by the coach. You want to appreciate the client's world – their hopes and fears, their aims and ambitions, their doubts and constraints – as fully as you can.

Another metaphor that I find useful in thinking about listening is the idea of 'Listening with the head' and 'Listening with the heart'. With the head, you hear facts and logic, costs and benefits, rational arguments. With the heart, you hear emotions. In a coaching conversation, when a client is exploring important issues in their life, there is often a strong emotional content. They may express this in words, but often it will be communicated non-verbally – in the look on their face, their body language or their tone of voice.

Note that it's not enough to listen to understand the client, it's also important to convey to the client that they've been listened to with empathy and without judgement. In my own practice, I find that simply playing back to the client a reasonably accurate understanding of what they've been communicating is often enough to enable them to move on in their thinking and perhaps action.

As I noted in the opening paragraph of this chapter, listening is important at two levels. First, it enables you as a coach to manage the conversation through questions, playback and so on. Second, and at a deeper level, listening builds the relationship between you and the client. We noted in Chapter 5, 'Emotional intelligence', this quote from Meg Wheatley:

> *Why is being heard so healing? I don't know the full answer to that question, but I do know that it has something to do with the fact that listening creates relationship.*
>
> (Wheatley, 2002)

Listening is an active process – it's much more than sitting passively while the other person talks. It's important to pay attention to both words and non-verbal communication. It requires concentration, and hence it can be tiring. I don't think that you can listen to understand all day long. Going back to the ladder of listening, there are times (outside coaching) when it's fine not to listen. I've certainly sat through meetings or agenda items when it was politically wise to be present but where paying attention to the discussion was pointless.

An important aspect of listening in a coaching context is silence. There are different types of silence. The client may be silent because they've nothing more to say about an aspect of the conversation. Or they may be confused or embarrassed or uncertain. And there are silences when they are busy thinking – it's usually easy to recognise that they've gone off into their head and are actively thinking things through. As a coach, you have a choice on whether or not to break a silence. If the client has finished exploring, or perhaps is feeling awkward in some way, you may choose to ask a question or offer a summary, for example, But, if the client if off thinking things through, don't interrupt the silence.

In her book *Fierce Conversations* Susan Scott, an executive coach, writes:

> *During my conversations with the people most important to me, silence has become my favourite sound, because that is when the work is being done. Of all the tools I use during conversations and all the principles I keep in mind, silence is the most powerful of all.*

(Scott, 2002)

There may be other times when, as a coach, it's appropriate to interrupt a client. Perhaps the client is sharing a lot of unnecessary detail. Or maybe it's near the end of a session and you want to focus them on some form of conclusion. It might be that the client is speaking as a way of avoiding what's really important to them, maybe a defence mechanism. You have a decision on what to say or do next in these situations, and you may choose to interrupt in order to manage and focus the conversation – in the interests of the client. If you do choose to interrupt, it's important to do it sensitively.

A final aspect of listening is listening to yourself. What thoughts are going through your head as the client speaks? How are you feeling? What seems to be the impact on the client of what you're doing? It can be useful to reflect in the moment on what's going on for you, and this may inform what you say or do next. In a later chapter, 'Use of self', we'll explore how as a coach you may use your self in your coaching conversations.

> **VIDEO**
>
> In this two-minute video, Nancy Kline shares some insightful thoughts on what she terms *'listening to ignite'*, contrasting this with *'listening to respond'*. She also highlights some poor coaching practice: https://conversational-leadership. net/listen-to-ignite/

## References

Scott, S (2002) *Fierce Conversations: Achieving Success in Work and in Life, One Conversation at a Time*. London: Piatkus.

Wheatley, M (2002) *Turning to One Another: Simple Conversations to Restore Hope to the Future*. San Francisco: Berrett-Koehler.

# Chapter 13: M

## MENTORING

There aren't standard, agreed definitions of coaching and of mentoring. When I worked in management development at the gas pipeline company Transco, one of my roles was to find external coaches for some the firm's directors and senior managers. One of the companies we partnered with for this was CPS, a prestigious firm with offices in Mayfair. They defined the terms more or less opposite to me, and regarded the service they provided to our executives as mentoring rather than coaching. Although this might have been confusing, it was clear that we wanted CPS mentors to coach our senior people.

Recall that my own definition of coaching, which underpins the text throughout this book, is:

*Coaching is a relationship of rapport and trust in which the coach uses their ability to listen, to ask questions and to play back what the client has communicated in order to help the client to clarify what matters to them and to work out what to do to achieve their aspirations.*

Here is my own, parallel definition of mentoring:

*Mentoring is a relationship in which the mentor draws on their experience, expertise and knowledge to support and guide a less experienced person in order to enhance their performance or encourage their development.*

Comparing my two definitions, I am positioning mentoring as being more towards the directive end of the spectrum, and coaching at the non-directive end. An effective mentor has relevant experience – for example, of an industry or an organisation or a role or a business problem – that is very relevant to the challenges which the mentee wants support on. Sharing their views can be of great value to the mentee.

I believe that a really effective mentor does this judiciously. They appreciate that the mentee is a different person with different priorities, and that the world isn't the same as it was, say, ten or 20 years ago. They select carefully when to share their thinking. And they also know when and how to operate non-directively, helping the mentee to choose their own way forward.

Someone once highlighted the difference between a coach and a mentor by saying that he could coach Barack Obama but he couldn't mentor Barack Obama. He could use his coaching skills if Obama was willing to be coached, but he couldn't mentor him as he'd never led a country. (I guess he might have been able to mentor Obama on how to bring up two children!)

Not everyone is suitable to be a mentor. Some very senior people – if they are autocratic or very judgemental or simply fascinated by the sound of their own voice – can be particularly unsuitable. A mentor must be able to build the right kind of relationship with their mentee. The mentor needs to be able to share their own experiences in a way that leaves the mentee free to take what they want to use and leave what they don't. They also need to be able to respect confidentiality. This can bring challenges if the mentor is a senior person within the same organisation as the mentee.

Warwick Business School (WBS) has a well-established and respected mentoring scheme in which alumni of WBS who have gone on to pursue their career in business act as mentors to current MBA students or recent graduates from WBS. The scheme has a dedicated (in both senses of the word) manager, Donna

Curtis. She ensures that there is a robust selection process – not everyone who applies to be a mentor is chosen. There is also a careful matching process to pair mentees up with an appropriate mentor. Each mentor receives initial training in coaching skills, and takes part in continuing professional development activities. The scheme is set up as a two-year mentoring relationship with a clear end point (although some relationships continue informally outside the scheme after this). If you are considering setting up a mentoring scheme within your own organisation, you may find the following pointers useful.

There are a number of situations where working with a supportive mentor can be particularly helpful. Mentoring can be valuable for someone who is taking on a significantly more senior role, or moving into an area where they have limited experience or joining an organisation from outside at a senior level. An organisation which has an effective talent management process may offer mentoring to the young people whom they see as having the potential to rise far. Mentoring can help people to break through real or perceived glass ceilings, helping not only the individual mentee but also promoting diversity within the organisation.

One question which may arise is whether or not a mentor within an organisation is a sponsor for their mentee. This is often a feature of mentoring in the United States. It can lead to issues of confidentiality, particularly if the mentoring arrangement is part of a talent management process in which directors assess together the progress of individuals. I recall one manager in Transco who was being mentored by one of our directors saying to me that he only shared things with his mentor that he was happy to be passed on to the rest of the directors. This will have severely constrained what was talked about and hence the value of the mentoring arrangement.

Although the primary purpose in a mentoring relationship is to help the mentee, there are a number of benefits in being a mentor. Mentors are playing a part in building the future capability of their organisation by developing some of its talented people. It provides a real-time opportunity for the mentor to practise and enhance their coaching skills. There is real satisfaction in helping another person to learn and grow in confidence and self-esteem. Seeing the world through the eyes of the mentee offers a fresh perspective, which might stimulate all sort of insights for the mentor. In a mentoring relationship, the mentor is a learner too!

**READING AND VIDEO**

Some organisations, industries or professions have their own mentoring scheme to support the development and career progression of their people. The webpage below contains details of one of these, the Royal College of General Practitioners' mentoring scheme. It includes a short video that sets out the benefits for both mentors and mentees of engaging in a mentoring relationship: www.rcgp.org.uk/training-exams/practice/rcgp-mentoring

# Chapter 14: N

## MAKING NOTES

In this chapter we look at the issue of making notes during a coaching conversation and reviewing these before the next session.

Coaches vary in their practice in regard to making notes. Some coaches don't make any notes at all during a session, often because they feel that this will get in the way of giving full attention to the client. At the other extreme, I've noticed that some people learning to coach take copious notes, perhaps in the belief that they may miss or forget something. I think that this does seriously risk not paying attention, and it certainly gets in the way of making eye contact with the client.

My own practice is to make sketchy notes, often just one word, to help me to register what seems important to the client. They may say something that I want to explore but I don't want to interrupt them. Jotting down a word or phrase helps me to remember to return to these. Sometimes a particular word or metaphor seems especially significant, and I may try to capture the exact words used by the client. In Chapter 29, 'Exploring metaphors', we'll consider how helping a client to investigate their metaphors can be powerful — noting the client's exact wording of a metaphor is useful here.

There are a couple of other times when I'm likely to make a note. First, when the client speaks near the start of the conversation about what they want to talk about today (Topic) and what they want to take away from this particular session (Outcome). Writing this down enables me to check as the session unfolds how well we're addressing these. I find this particularly helpful if the client says at the start that, for example, there are three things they want to speak about today. Second, there may be times when the client is making a list in response to a question I've asked. I may write down their answers so that I can play these back to the client. Alternatively, I may ask the client to write down the list – either while they speak or quietly on their own after they've finished speaking.

Clients occasionally ask if they can take away some notes I've made – perhaps, for example, I've sketched a model or diagram. I'm happy to give them my jottings. Sometimes I'll reassure a client that I'll tear up my notes at the end of the session. And there are times when the client is exploring very deeply an issue that's emotionally charged for them that it simply seems inappropriate or intrusive to make notes.

Some coaches also make notes after a session has ended. This can enable them to capture what seemed important to the client, perhaps what actions were agreed with the client, maybe what they wish to bring up with the client at the next session and possibly how the coach themself is thinking and feeling after the session. These notes may be a valuable resource for the coach to take to a session with their supervisor.

Clients have a legal right to see any notes you keep on them. If you do save notes, then write them in a way that would not embarrass you if a client saw them. *'Struggling in their new role'* may be a better way to phrase things than *'totally clueless'*.

Many coaches revisit their notes as they prepare for the next conversation with a client. This can remind them of things they want to say or ask in the session. It can also help them to tune in to the person whom they're about to speak with. This can be a valuable way of preparing, of leaving behind other matters or interferences, and focusing on the client they're about to meet.

I myself don't keep notes on my clients, and so don't have notes to read in preparation for a session. I treat each conversation as a separate encounter, and will ask the client near the start what they want to talk about. I leave it to the client to choose whether or not to revisit previous conversations or actions that they set out to do. One exception I make is in my role as a senior tutor for final year undergraduates at Warwick Business School. For each student I keep a password-protected document that records key points of my meetings with them. The students whom I see in this role are generally facing challenging circumstances that are interfering with their ability to study. I may need to refer to these notes in discussion with colleagues on the exam board when we're considering whether or not to make an adjustment to a student's final degree classification.

If you do make and keep notes of your conversations with a client, it's important to store these securely. The Global Code of Ethics, which has been agreed by a number of coaching bodies, including the Association for Coaching and the European Mentoring and Coaching Council, states:

> *Members will keep, store and dispose of all data and records of their client work including digital files and communications, in a manner that ensures confidentiality, security, and privacy, and complies with all relevant laws and agreements that exist in their client's country regarding data protection and privacy.*
>
> (Global Code of Ethics, 2021, p 5)

Some coaches send an email to a client after a session, noting what was agreed and what the client has said they'll do before the next session. I rarely do this, although I often email a model or an article that is relevant to what the client was discussing. Rather, I sometimes ask the client to drop me an email summarising either the key points they've taken from the conversation or the actions they've agreed to do. This might be because we've run out of time during the session to capture this. As discussed in Chapter 16, 'Playing back', I always leave the final summary at the end of a conversation with the client. The client's memory of what they've said or planned is more important than mine.

It can be helpful if a client gives some thought before a session to which issues they want to discuss. Capturing this in writing can be a simple way for a client to prepare for a session. I've noticed that some of my supervisees, in particular, do this diligently. Having heard – and noted down – the topics that the client wishes to discuss, I ask them which one they want to begin with. The client sets the agenda!

**REFLECTIVE TASK**

This exercise invites you to reflect upon your own practice in making notes and keeping records.

- What do you write down during a coaching session?
- What do you capture in writing after a session?
- What notes do you share with a client after a session?
- If you do keep notes, how do you store them securely?
- If you do keep notes, how do you review them before the next session?

You might like to consider if you wish to make any changes to your practice.

## Reference

Global Code of Ethics (2021) Global Code of Ethics for Coaches, Mentors, and Supervisors. [online] Available at: https://emccuk.org/ Common/Uploaded%20files/Policies/Global_Code_of_Ethics_EN_ v3.pdf (accessed 7 September 2022).

# Chapter 15: O

## I'M OK, YOU'RE OK

Thomas Harris' book *I'm OK, You're OK*, first published in 1967 and still in print, is a practical guide to Transactional Analysis. TA, as it's often referred to, is a psychological theory developed in the 1950s by Eric Berne. It seeks to explain how individuals think, feel, behave and interact with others, often in patterns that are repeated through life. It is a way of understanding what happens within and between people.

TA is fundamentally a psychoanalytic approach which assumes that our early childhood experiences profoundly shape – generally unconsciously – how we live our lives. Remembering that it's important as a coach to work within boundaries, I don't think it's appropriate to explore childhood experiences in any depth in a coaching context. However, it's possible to use some of the key ideas in TA at a cognitive level, helping a client to think differently about themselves, their behaviour and their relationships with others. One of the attractions of – and criticisms of – TA is that ideas are expressed in vivid and easily remembered language. In this chapter we look at some of the key ideas in Transactional Analysis.

A fundamental notion in TA is the idea of Parent, Adult and Child ego states. (TA uses initial capital letters here.) All of us spend time in each of these ego states. When we are in a Parent ego state, we're thinking, feeling and behaving in ways that we copied as a young child from our parents or other authority figures. When we are in a Child ego state, we're replaying in some sense how we thought, felt or behaved in our early years when we were seeking to gain the love or approval of our parents, or perhaps our siblings or carers. When we are in an Adult ego state, we are in the here and now, thinking clearly, in touch with our emotions and focused on what we are trying to do. This is generally a very resourceful state to operate from.

The Parent and Child ego states are subdivided. We can be in a *Nurturing Parent* ego state, where we are seeking to look after others, or we can be in a *Critical Parent* ego state, wagging our finger and telling others what they should be doing. We can be in a *Free Child* ego state, feeling playful, creative and having fun. Or we can be in an *Adapted Child* ego state, complying (perhaps unconsciously in ways that somehow reflect how we once adapted to gain love and approval from our parents) with the demands of others. The Adult ego state is not subdivided.

So far, in considering ego states, we have been concerned with the processes within an individual person. Transactional Analysis — as the name implies — is concerned with the communications or transactions between people and the relationships thereby created. One of the things that can happen in relationships is that we establish typical ways of interacting with one another. For example, a manager with a very directive, Command and Control style of managing may frequently be operating from a Critical Parent ego state. This may well engender Adapted Child responses from those who work for them. The typical pattern of interaction here is Parent–Child. Whole organisational cultures can be built on this basis.

Generally, an Adult–Adult relationship is more likely to be healthy and productive. To engage in an Adult–Adult conversation, you need to be straight in your communication and regard the other person as your equal simply because they are another human being (even though you may be more senior, experienced or talented). This is the basis of assertive communication.

The key to breaking a pattern of unhelpful Parent–Child transactions is to consistently communicate from an Adult ego state and to continually invite the other party to operate from their Adult (Figure 15.1). Note that there is no guarantee that the other party will respond from Adult – all you can do is to remain in Adult yourself and keep inviting an Adult response. Changing such an established pattern of interactions may well be difficult, not least because it requires the other party to change their behaviour, too.

**Figure 15.1  Parent–Child and Adult–Adult transactions**

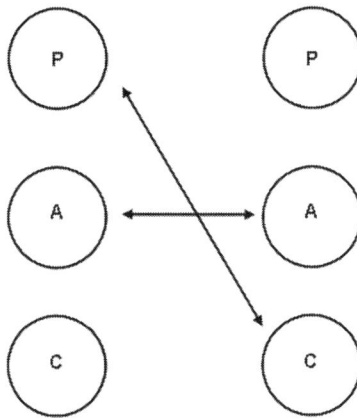

The idea of ego states and transactions is a framework that I often introduce to a client in a coaching conversation. For example, a client may be unhappy about how their line manager is treating them. It may be that their boss is typically operating from Critical Parent, and they are responding from Adapted Child. They may realise that their thinking and behaviour is reinforcing this pattern of relationship. They can then explore how to manage themself in order to stay in, and communicate from, an Adult ego state.

It's also a helpful framework to share with someone who finds it difficult to be assertive, either in a general sense or in a particular context where they behave passively. I like to distinguish between *basic assertiveness*, which is pushing for what you want, and *genuine assertiveness*, which is seeking to meet your needs and also the needs of the other party. Basic assertiveness is like a one-way street, whereas genuine assertiveness is a two-way street. Here is a definition of genuine assertiveness:

*Assertiveness is the ability to state clearly and confidently what you want or need in a situation and to allow the other party to state clearly what they want.*

Figure 15.2 contrasts being assertive with being passive, on the one hand, and being aggressive, on the other.

**Figure 15.2  Assertive, passive and aggressive behaviour**

**ASSERTIVE**

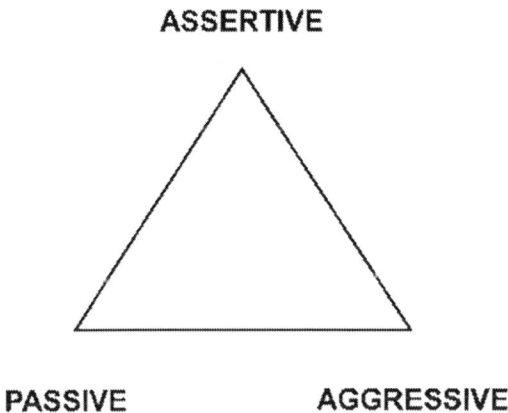

**PASSIVE**                    **AGGRESSIVE**

I find it interesting that it's people who are passive, not those who are aggressive, who sign up for workshops on assertiveness!

When someone is acting passively, it will often be the case that they are in an Adapted Child ego state. Consciously striving to remain in Adult, inviting the other person to respond from their Adult ego state, can help them to behave more assertively. If you are coaching someone in this situation, you might invite them to monitor themself in the situations that they find problematic, and review their experience with them at their next coaching session.

The title of Thomas Harris' book is based on the idea in TA of *life positions*. There are four life positions that reflect how a person sees the essential value in themselves and in others:

- **I'm OK, you're OK**. This is a *healthy* position, where the person feels good about themselves and others, seeks to collaborate, and finds it comfortable to behave assertively.
- **I'm not OK, you're OK**. This is a *depressive* position where the person feels one down on others and tends to behave passively.
- **I'm OK, you're not OK**. This is a *defensive* position where the person feels one up on others but behaves aggressively, competitively or insensitively to justify their stance. (There's an episode of *The Simpsons* where a character refers to a self-help book entitled *I'm OK, You're Sick and Twisted*.)
- **I'm not OK, you're not OK**. This is a *futile* position where the person considers that neither themselves nor others are any good, and often feels hopeless and helpless.

**VIDEO**

This five-minute video extends the discussion of Parent, Adult and Child ego states to consider how transactions might appear one way at a social level but actually be very different at a psychological level: www.youtube.com/watch?v=jetWN5UxReM

## Reference

Harris, T (2012) *I'm OK, You're OK*. London: Arrow Books.

# Chapter 16: P

## PLAYING BACK

Some of the books on coaching say that there are two key conversational skills – listening and questioning. For example, in *The Coach's Coach*, Alison Hardingham (2004) writes that, '*Questioning ... together with active listening probably achieves 80% of the positive outcome of coaching.*' Reflecting on my own practice, I believe that there is a third skill, which I call *playing back*. By this I mean playing back to the client what they've said or perhaps communicated non-verbally. I use playing back a lot in my coaching conversations.

There are three ways in which I play back. First, I might *summarise* what the client has been saying. This is usually about an extended piece of conversation. For instance, I might say something along the lines of '*So, there are three main things you're looking for In a new role: A, B and C.*' Hearing this summary may allow the client to clarify things. For instance, they might say that there's a fourth thing that matters to them, or perhaps that it's only really the first two that are important.

Second, I might *paraphrase* what the client says, turning their words into my own. For example, the client might say, '*I'm at the end of my tether*' and I respond with, '*Sounds like you're tired and maybe running out of hope.*' Hearing their words played back a bit differently is sometimes helpful for the client. They might reply, '*Yes, I'm beginning to feel hopeless. I hadn't realised that till now.*' However, there is a risk that, in modifying their language, my paraphrase isn't accurate. They might reply, '*No, I'm still feeling hopeful, just a bit frustrated today.*' I include words such as *'sounds like'* or *'maybe'* to indicate a degree of tentativeness in what I'm saying, giving the client space to correct me.

To avoid distorting what the client means, the third way in which I play back is to repeat the exact words used by the client. I call this *reflecting back.* In the previous example, I might respond by saying, *'Tell me more about being at the end of your tether.'* There are times when the precise wording used by the client is especially significant. It's helpful to listen for words that seem particularly vivid or meaningful. And sometimes the client will use a metaphor which conveys concisely and vividly what's really important to them. Inviting a client to explore a metaphor that is meaningful to them can be very helpful. In Chapter 29, 'Exploring metaphors', we'll look at the use of metaphor in coaching, and at an approach called Clean Language, which is based on helping the client to explore in depth and detail their metaphors and the exact words that they use.

Playing back – reasonably accurately – what the client has said has a number of important advantages. First, it enables you to check that you're understanding the client's position, and allows them to correct any misunderstanding. Second, it can be a good way to manage the conversation, perhaps providing a pause before moving the discussion on. A summary followed by a question is often a useful combination. Third, it also gives you time to think what to say or do next. Fourth, it shows the client that you've listened and understood what they've been discussing – feeling understood builds rapport and trust. This helps to deepen the relationship between coach and client. Recall that our definition begins *'Coaching is a relationship of rapport and trust ...'*

For a client, sometimes simply voicing to another person what matters is very helpful. Being heard, understood and accepted can be a powerful and validating experience. Such empathic understanding may be enough to enable the client to move on. In terms of the equation

Awareness + responsibility = performance

there are times when just enabling the client to become aware is all that's required. It may free them from something that's been troubling them, or it might make it obvious to them what they need to do.

It's also possible to play back something that the client has communicated non-verbally. Occasionally, you might mimic a gesture that seems significant – but take care to do this sensitively. Or you might say something along the lines of, '*I noticed when you spoke about your boss that your voice dropped and you seemed to slump in your chair.*' It's useful to play back what you noticed without interpreting what it means. Rather, invite the client to explore what it means for them.

One particular form of reflecting back is the idea of double-sided reflection. This is used in an approach called Motivational Interviewing to help a client who is feeling ambivalent about their situation. To offer a double-sided reflection, simply play back both halves of the client's dilemma or situation in a balanced way, without giving undue emphasis to one side or the other. For example, you might say, '*On the one hand, going to London offers excitement and possibilities. On the other hand, you'll be moving away from your friends and family.*'

While I use summarising, paraphrasing and reflecting back a lot during coaching conversations, I always leave the final summary with the client. Clients often feel surprised that I've asked them to summarise the conversation. I choose the wording of my invitation carefully. For example, if the client has created an action plan, I might say, '*As we draw to a close today, summarise what you're going to do.*' (This wording is also signalling that we're nearing the end of the conversation.) However, we may not have explored actions in the conversation, and such an invitation wouldn't be appropriate. So, I might say something along the lines of, *'Tell me what you're taking from today's conversation.'* It's often the case that what the client says has been important isn't what I would have highlighted. That's fine – it's what the client is taking from the conversation that matters, not what I thought was significant.

---

**REFLECTIVE TASK**

Here are two questions that invite you to summarise this chapter.

- What are the key ideas that you are taking from this chapter?
- What might you do differently in conversations as a result of reading this chapter?

---

## Reference

Hardingham, A (2004) *The Coach's Coach: Personal Development for Personal Developers*. London: Chartered Institute of Personnel and Development.

# Chapter 17: Q

## QUESTIONING

---

The three key conversational skills in coaching are listening, questioning and playing back. These work together, and good coaching questions emerge from listening with empathy to understand the client and their world. They follow the interests and the agenda of the client.

A very important distinction is that between *closed* and *open* questions. Closed questions can be answered *yes* or *no*, or perhaps with a one-word answer. Interestingly, closed questions generally begin with a verb, for example:

- Do you think that ...?
- Have you tried ...?
- Could you ...?

Open questions, on the other hand, invite a much fuller reply. To answer an open question, the client needs to do more thinking. Open questions are more likely to raise their awareness or encourage responsibility. And the answer to an open question is likely to reveal more information to the coach. Open questions begin with words like *what* or *how*, or phrases such as *'To what extent ...'* or *'In what ways ...'*.

Closed questions can usually be easily translated into an equivalent but more useful open question. For example, the above questions might become:

- What do you think?
- What have you tried?
- What options do you have?

Open questions are generally much more useful in coaching. However, occasionally, a closed question is appropriate. For example, you might wish to invite the client to make a decision or commitment, asking something like, *'So, are you going to do X?'* Or you might wish to move the conversation on, perhaps to the next stage of the GROW model, by asking, for example, *'Are you ready to move on to explore options?'*

I often use a short phrase, such as *'Tell me about ...'* or *'Say a bit more about ...'*, to encourage a client to explore further. I regard such phrases as equivalent to an open question.

One type of open question that can be problematic are those beginning with *why*. We shall explore these in Chapter 30, 'Why?'

Another important feature of good coaching questions is that they are short and focused. The word I like to use here is *crisp*. It's usually possible to ask a clear and helpful question in half a dozen words or so. For example, *'What is bothering you?'* or *'What would success look like?'* or *'How might you do that?'*

The actual wording of a question is important. It's often worth taking a few moments to clarify in your own mind your next question, taking into account what you think will be most helpful for the client at that point. This is better than starting to speak without being clear what you want to ask. This can lead to long questions or to multiple questions when the coach asks four or five questions one after the other. People sometimes ask a question and then go on to justify it or explain why they're asking it – which may mean that the other person has forgotten what the question was when the questioner stops talking. Long or multiple questions are likely to confuse the client.

As discussed in the chapter on the GROW model, I like to ask two questions near the start of a coaching conversation, which modify the framework to become TO GROW. To establish the focus for the conversation, I ask two questions along the lines of:

**T**opic What do you want to talk about today?

**O**bjective What would be a useful outcome from this conversation?

Another type of question that I use often is '*What else?*' I'm inviting the client to consider if there's anything else that's relevant to whatever aspect we've been exploring. I generally explain that I'm not suggesting that there should be something else. I sometimes use the phrase '*Is there anything else?*' I think that the word *anything* makes this a semi-open rather than a closed question, although grammatically it is indeed a closed question.

One form of question that can be useful is a *scaling* question, where you ask the client to rate something that's relevant to what they're exploring on a scale from one to ten – where ten is the top of the scale. Again, the wording is important. Here are some examples that have a different focus:

- On a scale from one to ten, how committed are you to …?
- On a scale from one to ten, how confident are you about …?
- On a scale from one to ten, how anxious are you feeling?

This type of question can help to focus the client's thoughts or feelings. A useful follow-up question is to ask them what it would take to be one point higher on the scale (or one point lower, in the case of the third question above). I don't think it's helpful, if the client is at a low or mid-point on the scale, to ask them what it would take to be at ten – that's probably too big a leap.

One type of question to avoid in coaching is a *leading* question – that is, one that already contains the answer. Here are a couple of examples:

- Do you think it would be a good idea to do X?
- Have you considered doing Y?

These are effectively suggestions. I think it is better to be clear in your own mind that you want to offer a suggestion, and to state the suggestion clearly. You might reword these two leading questions along these lines:

- I think that doing X might be a good idea. What do you think?
- I wonder if you've considered doing Y. What's your view?

There may be times when you find yourself asking a series of questions, generating short answers. This might be because you're asking too many closed questions. But it could be because the client isn't really engaging in the conversation. It may begin to feel a bit like an interrogation, and you as the coach might feel that you're doing most of the work in the conversation. If that's the case, then do something different! For example, you might invite the client to write something down. Or you could ask them to draw a picture. Or, depending on how well-established your relationship is with this client, you might name what you're experiencing, perhaps saying something along the lines of, '*I seem to be asking a lot of questions today which you're answering very briefly. I wonder what's going on.*' Your tone of voice is likely to be important here.

**REFLECTIVE TASK**

Here are three things that you might do over, say, the next week or so to observe and reflect upon the questions that you and others ask.

- Watch or listen to some current affairs programmes on TV or radio. Notice how often an interviewer asks long questions, multiple questions or leading questions. How does the interviewee respond? (Note that politicians are professionally trained to answer the question that they want to answer, which is unlikely to be the question posed.)
- Observe the questions that others ask in meetings or conversation with you. Who asks short, open questions? Who asks long or multiple questions? What then happens?
- Pay attention to the questions that you yourself ask. Rate these on a scale from one (long and unclear) to ten (open and crisp). What is the effect of your questions?

# Chapter 18: R

## COACHING AS A RELATIONSHIP

Throughout the book we have been working with a definition of coaching which begins with the words *'Coaching is a relationship of rapport and trust.'* In this chapter we consider the views of a number of authors on the nature of an effective coaching relationship.

My approach to coaching owes much to the person-centred approach to therapy and counselling of Carl Rogers. As we discussed in Chapter 4, *'Don't Just Do Something, Sit There'*, Rogers sets out three core conditions that the therapist or counsellor needs to convey to the client. He regards these as both necessary and sufficient to enable the client to grow and develop.

- Unconditional positive regard, also termed non-judgemental acceptance, for the client (we looked at this in the chapter on judgement).
- Empathic understanding.
- Congruence – the coach being real and genuine.

If a therapist or counsellor can offer a relationship characterised by these core conditions, then the client is enabled to tap into their own resources (which Rogers refers to as their *'self-actualizing tendency'*) in order to understand themself, to alter their sense of self, to modify their attitudes and to change their behaviour. As a coach, I similarly aim to offer a relationship based on these three core conditions.

Counsellors working from a Rogerian stance don't generally offer advice, guidance or suggestions. Rather, they focus on playing back an empathic and acceptant understanding to the client. I once met an experienced Rogerian counsellor on a coaching programme who found it really difficult to ask questions because, from her perspective, questioning was too directive.

In Chapter 8, '*How to Coach*', we summarised the views set out by Erik de Haan from his meta-analysis of the research into how psychotherapy works. We noted his conclusion that, '*The only thing the coach can actually influence … is the* relationship *between coach and coachee*' (de Haan, 2008, emphasis in original).

De Haan notes the similarities between his views and Carl Rogers' person-centred approach. However, he takes a very different view on being directive. He believes that a coach can:

> *just as easily make use of more directive, suggestive and confronting interventions, precisely because I assume that the coachee can take it; or in fact that even the strongest confrontations, prescriptions and provocations are generally not powerful enough to unbalance the ability of coachees to change themselves, or to establish it if this is lacking.*
>
> (de Haan, 2008)

So, while both de Haan and Rogers emphasise the importance of the relationship in helping a client to grow, they take very different positions whether or not to operate from the directive end of the spectrum. You might like to reflect on what your own approach is in this regard.

In Chapter 15, '*I'm OK, You're OK*', we looked at the idea from Transactional Analysis of Parent, Adult and Child ego states, and how these can explain relationships that are characterised by

Parent–Child transactions or by Adult–Adult transactions. One risk in operating from the directive end of the spectrum, offering advice and suggestions, is that it may lead to a relationship between a coach who is operating from their Nurturing Parent with a client who is acting from their Adapted Child. This might create a dependence on the coach. And it may, while offering short-term help and solutions, be much less developmental for the client. My own view is that an Adult–Adult relationship will be much more empowering, enabling the client to make their own choices to pursue their aspirations with due regard to any concerns or constraints that they have.

My definition views coaching as a relationship of rapport and trust. Developing rapport and trust may take time. The client might be willing to share things with you in the fourth session that they weren't ready to share at the beginning because they've learnt through your work together that they can trust you, that you are in their corner, that you have their best interests at heart. As trust grows, so too does rapport. And as rapport builds, trust develops.

While it's important that the client trusts the coach, if you're operating from a primarily non-directive perspective it's important too that the coach trusts the client – to work out what they want and what they are prepared to do to achieve their aims.

Myles Downey writes these words to emphasise the central importance of the relationship in coaching. (*Player* is his word for *client* or *coachee*.)

> *Effective coaching rests on a solid relationship between coach and player*

> *Without a relationship there is no coaching. In fact the only real mistake that a coach can make is to damage the relationship irreparably. Everything else is recoverable.*

> (Downey, 2003)

Another aspect of a strong coaching relationship is the balance between support and challenge that the coach offers the client. It's vital that the client feels supported by the coach. I think it's important that the client feels support before offering challenge. Alison Hardingham discusses a number of roles that a coach may play, including the role of challenger. She writes:

> *Deciding how often, and when, to take the role of challenger is one of the key things a coach must pay attention to. She needs to observe carefully the effect her challenging has. Does it liberate the coachee from some behaviour he had got stuck in? Or does it mire him in uncertainty and passivity?*
>
> (Hardingham, 2004)

In their book, which has the title *Challenging Coaching*, John Blakey and Ian Day take the view that coaching needs to incorporate a high degree of challenge as well as support, and that clients welcome and thrive on being challenged. They write that:

> *a healthy challenge, when delivered from a relationship of trust and mutual respect, serves to stretch people's thinking and drives them to dig deeper into the reality of their situation and the true potential of the future.*
>
> (Blakey and Day, 2012)

I believe that it's possible to offer challenge to a client without being directive. As an illustration, you might use the idea of double-sided reflection, which we looked at in Chapter 16, 'Playing back', to say something along these lines to a client: '*You've said over the last few sessions that you are keen to find a new job. Yet, you haven't revised your CV or applied for any positions. I wonder how these sit together?*'

**VIDEO**

This four-minute video discusses some practical steps to build trust in a coaching relationship, and notes some behaviours that destroy trust. It also mentions extra challenges here for a line manager seeking to coach one of their people: www.youtube.com/watch?v=zMNyhgsx2h8

## References

Blakey, J and Day, I (2012) *Challenging Coaching: Going Beyond Traditional Coaching to Face the Facts.* London: Nicholas Brealey.

de Haan, E (2008) *Relational Coaching: Journeys Towards Mastering One-to-One Learning*. Chichester: John Wiley.

Downey, M (2003) *Effective Coaching: Lessons from the Coach's Coach*. London: Texere.

Hardingham, A (2004) *The Coach's Coach: Personal Development for Personal Developers*. London: Chartered Institute of Personnel and Development.

# Chapter 19: S

## SUPERVISION

The Global Code of Ethics (2021, p 8), agreed by a number of coaching bodies including the Association for Coaching and the European Mentoring and Coaching Council, includes this statement:

*Members will engage in supervision with a suitably qualified/experienced supervisor and peer supervision with a level of frequency that is appropriate to their coaching, mentoring or supervision practice, the requirements of their professional body and level of accreditation, and have evidence of engagement in reflective practice.*

If you are doing a reasonable amount of coaching, it is good practice to engage in appropriate supervision. This provides a vehicle to reflect upon and enhance your practice as a coach. We'll consider later in the chapter different forms of supervision.

In his book *The Coaching Relationship in Practice*, Geoff Pelham offers a clear and practical definition of supervision:

*Coaching supervision is primarily about providing a safe reflective space where you can share your practice with someone who knows about coaching and is often more experienced in the field, with the intention of deepening your understanding of coaching and developing your capability to work more effectively. It is also a place to contain and work through the anxieties, uncertainties and confusions that arise in coaching.*

(Pelham, 2016)

In their book *Coaching, Mentoring and Organizational Consultancy*, Peter Hawkins and Nick Smith (2006) distinguish three functions of supervision.

1. The *developmental* function is about developing the skills, understanding and capacities of the supervisee, through reflection on their practice.
2. The *resourcing* function is about helping the supervisee to become aware of and deal with their reactions to the emotional intensity of their work with clients.
3. The *qualitative* function provides quality control of the work of the supervisee, ensuring that the work is appropriate and ethical.

In my own experience as a supervisor, I find that supervisees sometimes wish to explore a fourth function not listed above.

4. The *business development* function is about helping the supervisee to explore commercial issues and what they will do to build their coaching business.

Just as the GROW model is widely known in the coaching world, there is also a key framework in supervision, the *seven-eyed model*, which was developed by Peter Hawkins and Robin Shohet (2006) (see Figure 19.1 for a summary). In a supervision conversation with a supervisee I can invite them to reflect from seven different perspectives or modes or eyes. I've illustrated these below with some typical questions or statements for each mode.

- **Mode 1: Focus on the client and how they present**
  Tell me about the client.
  What issues did they bring to the session?

- **Mode 2: Exploration of the strategies and interventions used by the coach with the client**
  What tools or exercises did you use in the last session?
  What might you do in the next session?

- **Mode 3: Exploration of the relationship between the client and the coach**
  What words characterise the relationship between you and the client?
  If it was working even more effectively, what would be different about the relationship?

- **Mode 4: Focus on the coach**
  What are you thinking when you are with this client?
  How do you feel about this client?

- **Mode 5: Focus on the relationship between the coach and the supervisor**
  We seem to be jumping from topic to topic in this session – I wonder why that might be.
  How might what's happening between us in this conversation parallel what goes on between you and the client in your sessions?

- **Mode 6: The supervisor focusing on their own process – what is going for them, here and now**
  As you're speaking today, I'm feeling confused – I wonder what that might mean.
  Let me share with you an image that's just come into my head.

- **Mode 7: Focus on the wider context in which the coaching happens**
  What factors in the client's organisation are affecting their situation?
  What aspects of the business environment seem particularly relevant to the situation that the client is in?

**Figure 19.1 The seven-eyed supervision model**

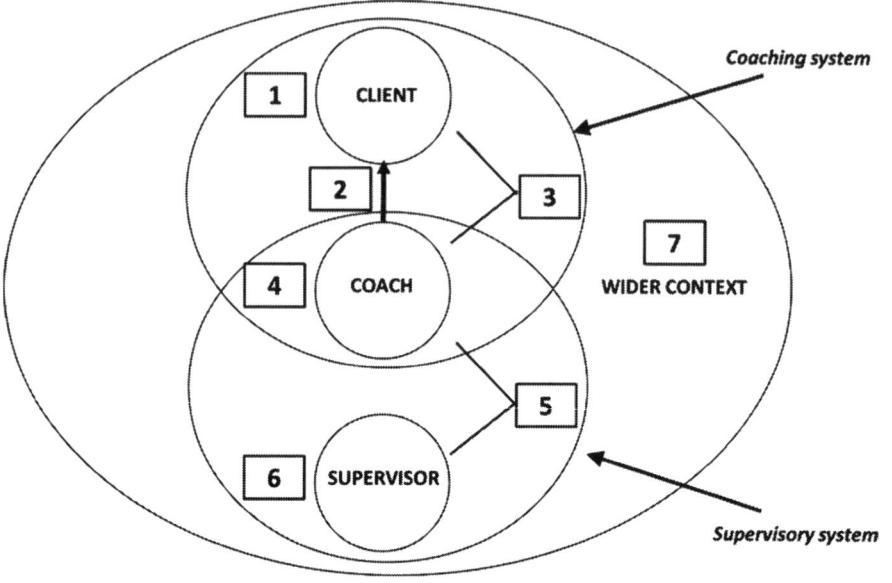

There usually isn't time in a single session to work in all seven modes. I find it helpful to have the model at the back of my mind, helping me to choose what to say or do next. A question that I particularly like which bridges a number of the modes is *What does this client need from you?*

There are a number of forms that a supervision arrangement might take. First, a coach might work one-to-one with their supervisor. At the moment, this is the type of supervision that I have. I have the good fortune to be supervised by Tatiana Bachkirova, a very experienced coach, supervisor and author of many books and articles. Second, two or three coaches might work together to supervise each other in a *co-supervision* agreement. This has the advantage that it is likely to be free rather than paid for. It also enables learning from the roles of supervisee, supervisor and, in a trio, of observing a supervision session. It might be particularly suitable for participants on a coaching course who are still developing their practice. Third, a coach might take part with other coaches in *group supervision* where a supervisor works with a number of coaches in a joint session. This is also likely to be cheaper than one-to-one supervision. It also enables individual coaches to learn from one another. A downside is that the time that each individual coach has to explore their own agenda is limited. It is also possible to combine these forms – for instance, a coach working as part of a team of coaches might have group supervision with their colleagues as well as individual supervision with a different supervisor.

It is a good idea to think before a supervision session which clients or themes you wish to explore in the conversation. I ask each of my supervisees near the start of our sessions what they want to discuss today, and this gives a clear agenda for the conversation. My supervisor, Tatiana Bachkirova, has a one-page Word template that I complete and email to her ahead of each session. I also find it useful to capture my learning points or key takeaways after each of my sessions with her.

It's also a good idea to review from time to time how the supervision is going – what's working well and what might be done differently. This can also help the supervisee to consider when it might be time to move on to working with a different supervisor.

---

**REFLECTIVE TASK**

In Chapter 7, 'The GROW model', I shared an exercise called *silent coaching* which I use in workshops to introduce the framework. I also use an exercise called *silent supervision* in workshops to introduce the seven-eyed supervision model. You might like to try out the exercise to reflect upon one of your clients through five of the seven eyes. I don't think it's possible to replicate modes five and six in such an exercise since there isn't a supervisor present.

**Mode one**
- Who is the client you wish to reflect upon?
- Describe the client.
- What issues are they mainly concerned with?

**Mode seven**
- What factors in the client's organisation seem to be especially relevant to them?
- What issues in the wider business environment are affecting them?

**Mode two**
- What interventions have you used with this client?
- And what has been the effect of these interventions?

**Mode four**
- What do you think about this client?
- How do you feel about this client?

**Mode three**
- What words characterise the relationship between you and this client?
- How would you like the relationship to be different?

**Mode two**
- *(It is often useful to return to mode two at the end of a supervision conversation.)*
- What will you do differently next time you are with this client?

## References

Global Code of Ethics (2021) Global Code of Ethics for Coaches, Mentors, and Supervisors. [online] Available at: https://emccuk.org/Common/Uploaded%20files/Policies/Global_Code_of_Ethics_EN_v3.pdf (accessed 7 September 2022).

Hawkins, P and Shohet, R (2006) *Supervision in the Helping Professions*. Maidenhead: Open University Press.

Hawkins, P and Smith, N (2006) *Coaching, Mentoring and Organizational Consultancy: Supervision, Skills and Development*. Maidenhead: Open University Press.

Pelham, G (2016) *The Coaching Relationship in Practice*. London: Sage.

# Chapter 20: T

## COACHING A TEAM

The use of coaching with a team of people has been growing over recent years. In his book *Coaching the Team at Work*, David Clutterbuck offers this definition of team coaching:

*Helping the team improve performance, and the processes by which performance is achieved, through reflection and dialogue.*

(Clutterbuck, 2007)

Over the years I have facilitated many away days where a team has gathered, usually either to improve how they are working together or to consider their strategy. These are often one-off events. I regard this as facilitation rather than coaching. David Clutterbuck clarifies the distinction:

*The purpose of facilitation is to provide external dialogue management to help the team reach complex or difficult decisions. The purpose of coaching is to empower the team to manage its own dialogue, in order to enhance its capability and performance.*

(Clutterbuck, 2007)

The aim of the team coach is to enable the team to be self-sufficient, able to use coaching techniques skilfully to address issues and challenges when the coach isn't present. Team coaching is about enabling a team to:

- clarify and achieve their collective goals;
- communicate and interact with one another effectively;
- constructively explore and resolve differences within the team;

- make wise decisions;
- engage effectively with key stakeholders outside the team.

Just because a group of people sit in the same office or report to the same director, this doesn't mean that they are – or need to be – a genuine team. I find the definition offered by Jon Katzenbach and Douglas Smith in their book *The Wisdom of Teams* a really useful way of distinguishing between a group and a team. Each word or phrase in the definition has been carefully chosen and is meaningful:

> *A team is a small number of people with complementary skills committed to a common purpose, performance goals and ways of working together for which they hold themselves mutually accountable.*

(Katzenbach and Smith, 1994)

Another common myth in regard to teams is the idea that, to develop as a high-performing team, a group needs to go through phases of *Forming*, *Storming*, *Norming* and *Performing*. Bruce Tuckman created the model in 1965 based on a survey he carried out of 50 articles on group development. Three-quarters of these articles were about therapy groups or encounter groups (which were popular at that time). It's not at all clear to me that a group of people reporting to a line manager within an organisation will go through the same phases as a therapy group. I think the popularity of the framework – and it is probably the best-known model of group development – owes much to the memorability of the mnemonic.

I prefer the model that John Whitmore describes in his book *Coaching for Performance* (2002). He suggests that teams go through three stages.

1. *Inclusion* – people may be feeling insecure, and assessing to what extent they are included in the group.

2. *Assertion* – those who feel included assert themselves, seeking to establish their place in the group and perhaps the pecking order. There may be competition, and sometimes this can be very productive.
3. *Co-operation* – people who feel secure in their place have the space to support and trust others. There is commitment. There may also be disagreement, but this is worked through constructively.

One feature that I like about this model is that it recognises that different people might be in different places. The model also recognises that groups may move back and forwards. For example, a team that is cooperative may slip back – perhaps because the environment changes, or maybe because someone leaves or joins the group.

Many of the ideas that we've been exploring in relation to the coaching of individuals translate easily into the coaching of teams. The basic equation that is at the heart of coaching also applies in team coaching.

Awareness + responsibility = performance

The GROW framework for structuring a coaching conversation with an individual client can also be applied to conversations involving the members of a team. Because different individuals are likely to have varying views, there may need to be more discussion to reach agreement on what the *Goal* of the team is in relation to a particular issue. Similarly, there are likely to be diverse views on what is happening in the current *Reality* of the team. And making a decision that has genuine commitment on what *Will* be done is likely to be more challenging for a group than for an individual. It may take considerable time to reach consensus, or the team leader may make the decision, or possibly a vote might be taken to choose between different Options. The *Options* phase of the GROW model is one area where the varying perspectives of individuals is useful in creating a range of possibilities to choose from.

The fact that there are a number of people taking part in a team coaching conversation poses extra challenges for the coach as they seek to manage a constructive dialogue. There may also be unhealthy dynamics, rivalries or conflict among the members of the group – these may or may not be expressed, and indeed might be unconscious. To manage the conversation when there are complex dynamics within the group, it can be useful if two coaches work together. One coach may take a back seat, as it were, to observe what's going on, intervening when it's appropriate. And, of course, this observer role can be swapped between the two coaches. In *The Coach's Coach*, Alison Hardingham writes:

> *And if the group dynamic in a team is very powerful and very destructive, it may be better for coaching to be done by a team of two coaches working together. It is much easier to resist the power of group dynamics when there is more than one of you.*

(Hardingham, 2004)

Let's conclude by revising a point made near the start of the chapter, that the team coach is aiming to enable the team to be self-sufficient. To put this in other words, the aim is to help the team to learn how to coach itself – to become a self-coaching team. David Clutterbuck (2007) writes that a self-coaching team:

- finds the difficult questions, wherever they are;
- tracks down new knowledge;
- adapts and leads the coaching process;
- generates its own feedback, internally and from others;
- motivates itself to learn.

He concludes that the ultimate goal of the team coach is self-sufficiency, when the team can '*apply coaching techniques with skill and insight into its own issues, in its own way and in its own time*' (Clutterbuck, 2007).

**REFLECTIVE TASK**

You might use this exercise in working as a coach or as a facilitator with a group or team. To try it out for yourself, think about a group that you work in or with – or perhaps engage with outside of a work context. It's best if the group isn't bigger than ten people – in their research, Katzenbach and Smith (1994) found that most of the effective groups they studied had fewer than ten members.

**Figure 20.1  A model of team development**

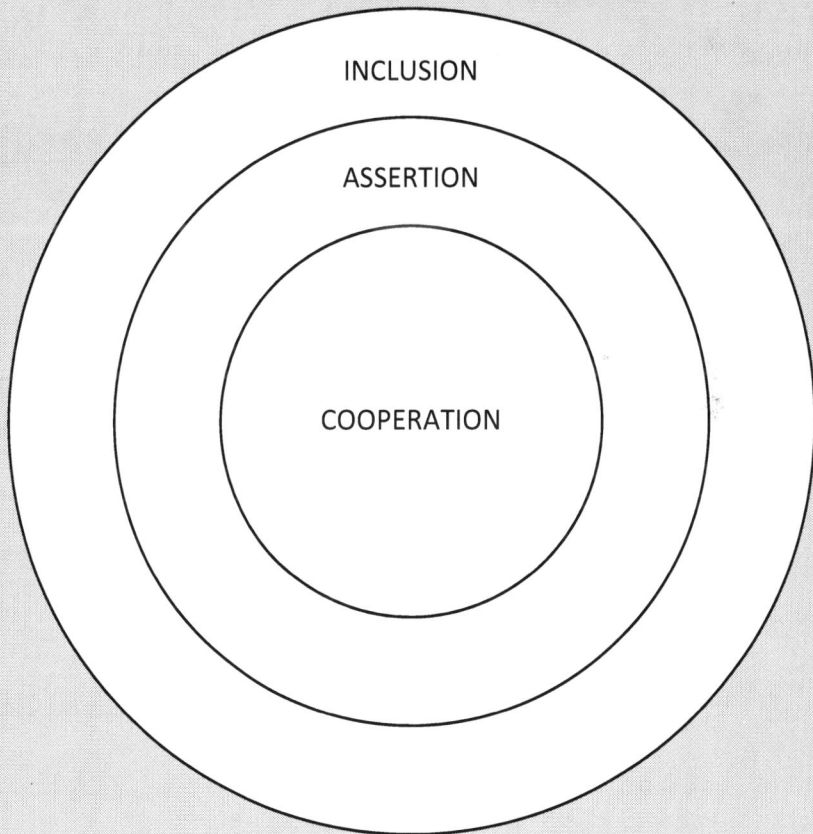

INCLUSION

ASSERTION

COOPERATION

$\rightarrow$

On Figure 20.1 write the names of each member of the group according to whether they seem to be:

- At the *Inclusion* stage – not secure of their position in the group and wondering where they fit.
- At the *Assertion* stage – staking a claim for their contribution and their place in the pecking order.
- At the *Cooperation* stage – committed to the group, feeling confident of their place and supporting other members of the group.
- What strikes you when you look at where you've positioned the individuals?

If you are using the exercise with a group, it can be helpful to explore with them where different people seem to be. You might also explore diverse perspectives on where individuals have placed people.

## References

Clutterbuck, D (2007) *Coaching the Team at Work*. London: Nicholas Brealey.

Hardingham, A (2004) *The Coach's Coach: Personal Development for Personal Developers*. London: Chartered Institute of Personnel and Development.

Katzenbach, J and Smith, D (1994) *The Wisdom of Teams: Creating the High-Performance Organization*. New York: Harper.

Tuckman, B (1965) Developmental Sequence in Small Groups. *Psychological Bulletin*, 63(6): 384–99.

Whitmore, J (2002) *Coaching for Performance: The Principles of Coaching and Leadership*. London: Nicholas Brealey.

# Chapter 21: U

## *UNDERSTANDING YOURSELF AND OTHERS*

My book *Understanding Yourself and Others*, which was published in 2014, has the subtitle *Practical Ideas from the World of Coaching*. In it, I set out a number of ideas, theories and models that I'd been using in my work as a coach and in designing learning and development workshops and programmes. Since then, I've found the book a rich resource to share ideas and frameworks with my coaching clients. During a coaching or supervision conversation, I often discuss with a client a model that hopefully offers them a helpful way of thinking about the issue they're exploring. In terms of the directive to non-directive spectrum, this is shifting towards the directive end. However, I try to make clear to the client that a model is simply a perspective that may or may not be helpful, leaving it up to them to make sense of it or simply to discard it. I usually follow up by sending an email to the client, attaching some text from my book that explains the model, perhaps in more detail.

In your own practice, what is your view of sharing a theory or model with a client?

Here is the list of chapter headings from the book.

1. Coaching and learning from experience
2. Emotional intelligence
3. Understanding your personality type
4. Ideas from Transactional Analysis
5. Conversations

6. Assertiveness and handling conflict
7. Influencing
8. Managing your time
9. Achieving things through other people
10. Taking part in or chairing meetings
11. Coping with and introducing change

I discuss some of these ideas elsewhere in this book – for instance, in the chapters 'Emotional intelligence', '*I'm OK, You're OK*', 'Extraverts and Introverts' and 'Time management'. In this chapter, we look at some ideas on handling conflict and on change.

Kenneth Thomas and Ralph Kilmann (1974) have a very useful model, summarised in Figure 21.1, which shows five ways of approaching conflict. It's based on whether you seek to satisfy your own needs or the needs of the other party.

**Figure 21.1 The Thomas-Kilmann conflict handling framework**

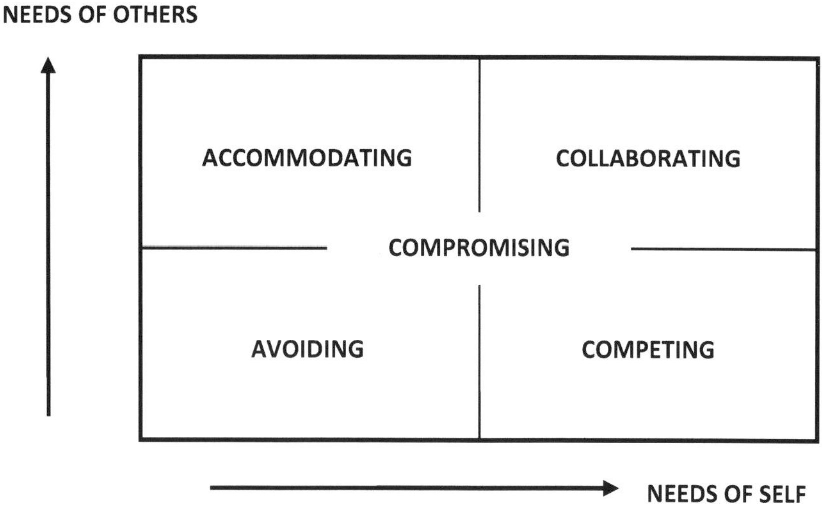

NEEDS OF OTHERS

```
         ┌─────────────────┬─────────────────┐
         │                 │                 │
         │  ACCOMMODATING  │  COLLABORATING  │
         │                 │                 │
         │         COMPROMISING              │
         │                 │                 │
         │    AVOIDING     │    COMPETING    │
         │                 │                 │
         └─────────────────┴─────────────────┘
                                    ───────────▶ NEEDS OF SELF
```

This leads to five possible approaches.

1. Seeking to satisfy your own needs with little or no regard to the needs of the other person is *competing*.

2. Prioritising the needs of the other party and disregarding your own needs is *accommodating*.
3. Making no effort to address the needs of either of you is *avoiding*.
4. Seeking to find a way to satisfy both your own needs and the needs of the other person is *collaborating*.
5. Looking to meet some of your needs and some of the other party's – splitting the difference in some way – is *compromising*.

Note that each of these can be useful in different contexts. Sometimes it's best to avoid the issue – perhaps for the time being. Sometimes a genuinely collaborative solution isn't possible, and it might be better to compromise.

I like the definition of conflict as *'any form of disagreement however large or small'*. In a healthy, high-performing team, there is conflict – and this gets explored so that agreements are reached on the way forward. In a less healthy or well-developed team, there is conflict but it isn't discussed and so no resolution is achieved – the conflict is avoided.

In the final chapter of *Understanding Yourself and Others*, 'Coping with and introducing change', I summarise a number of relevant models, including Elizabeth Kübler-Ross' model of five stages of grief (Kübler-Ross, 1969) and Abraham Maslow's hierarchy of needs (Maslow, 1954). (Incidentally, Kübler-Ross never represented her framework as a curve, and Maslow never represented his hierarchy as a pyramid!) Another idea that I sometimes share with a coaching client is William Bridges' distinction between change and *transition*. Change, he argues, is a shift in the externals of a situation. Transition, on the other hand, is the emotional and psychological *'process that people go through as they internalize and come to terms with the details of the new situation that the change brings about'* (Bridges, 1991). Understanding and taking account of transition is vital if you want to make sense of how you yourself are responding to a change or if you want to support others through change.

Transition consists of three phases – the ending, the neutral zone and the beginning. Paradoxically, it starts with ending and finishes with beginning.

1. In the *ending* phase, each individual involved is trying to understand what has ended and to face up to the nature of their loss. They may be afraid of the unknown. It is important to appreciate that this will result in resistance. Some people can become stuck in this phase. Bridges (1991) advises that you will save yourself a lot of trouble if you remember that the *'first task of transition management is to convince people to leave home'*.
2. In the *neutral* zone, the old way has ended but the new way is not established. This phase is characterised by uncertainty, disorientation, confusion and discomfort. However, Bridges suggests that in this phase there may be tremendous opportunity to create new ways of thinking and working.
3. In the *beginning* phase, certainty returns. People discover new energy, new purpose and new identity. The new way of working feels comfortable, and may even seem like the only possible way.

Note that these three stages may not be sharply delineated, and different people will move forward at different paces.

If the idea of introducing a model or theory to clients appeals to you, you might reflect on the frameworks that you yourself find useful in different contexts. And you might explore what other frameworks you'd like to know more about in order to help your clients to make sense of and to tackle the challenges they bring to coaching. While I find the material in the chapters listed above really useful, there are also times when I'll do a quick internet search to identify a suitable resource to send to a client after a session.

**VIDEOS**

This three-minute video describes the five conflict handling styles in the Thomas-Kilmann framework, and notes situations where each may be appropriate: www.youtube.com/watch?v=HxgSjnWSzf8

This six-minute video offers a number of ideas for anyone introducing change on how to help people to navigate the three phases of the Bridges' transition model: www.youtube.com/watch?v=3Gm9bEGp4mY

# References

Bridges, W (1991) *Managing Transitions: Making the Most of Change*. Reading, MA: Addison-Wesley.

Kübler-Ross, E (1969) *On Death and Dying*. New York: Macmillan.

Maslow, A (1954) *Motivation and Personality*. New York: Harper.

Thomas, K and Kilmann R (1974) *Thomas-Kilmann Conflict Mode Instrument*. Mountain View: Xicom.

Thomson, B (2014) *Understanding Yourself and Others: Practical Ideas from the World of Coaching*. London: Sheldon Press.

# Chapter 22: V

## VOICING

In earlier chapters we have looked at the three key conversational skills in coaching – listening to understand, asking crisp, open questions and playing back an empathic understanding. There is a fourth skill – voicing assertively your thoughts, feelings and wants – which is essential in order to take part in high-quality conversations. Whereas the first three coaching skills are focused on understanding the other party, voicing is about putting your views into a conversation or meeting.

Voicing is the ability to state clearly what you think and the reasons that underlie your thinking. This is at the heart of behaving assertively. And it is very useful for anyone wishing to operate from their Adult ego state, inviting an Adult response from the other person.

In her book *Fierce Conversations*, Susan Scott (2002) writes about conversations that get to the heart of the matter. *Fierce* doesn't mean aggressive, but rather robust, passionate and authentic. Fierce conversations surface assumptions, explore different perspectives, and seek collaborative outcomes that satisfy both parties.

This type of conversation takes time – and skill. However, avoiding these conversations means that important issues don't get addressed. Politely discussing the issues is likely to mean that there's no real commitment to actions to tackle things effectively. Susan Scott (2002) writes that, *'fierce conversations often do take time. The problem is, anything else takes longer.'*

In their book *Difficult Conversations*, Douglas Stone, Bruce Patton and Sheila Heen explore how to have those tough conversations that matter most. They write that:

> *When we fail to share what's important to us, we detach ourselves from others and damage our relationships.*
>
> *A relationship takes hold and grows when both participants experience themselves and the other as being authentic.*
>
> (Stone et al, 1999)

Engaging in difficult or fierce conversations isn't easy. The issue is likely to be important, at least to one party and perhaps to both. And there are likely to be strong emotions in play. Stone et al (1999) suggest that a difficult conversation is actually three conversations.

1. The 'What happened?' conversation: Most difficult conversations involve disagreements about what has happened or what should happen.
2. The *feelings* conversation: Every difficult conversation also asks and answers questions about feelings. These feelings may not be addressed directly, but they will leak in anyway.
3. The *identity* conversation: This is the conversation we each have with ourselves about what this situation means to us. The situation underlying the difficult conversation might cause us to question whether, for example, we are as supportive a manager as we believed we were.

They suggest that one way of engaging effectively in a difficult conversation is to move from a conversation about who is to blame to a conversation that is focused on learning for next time.

A blame conversation is about trying to prove that you are right and the other person is wrong – it's about winning and losing. A learning conversation is about sharing and about seeking to understand each other's perspectives, aiming to construct a way forward that will benefit both parties. You might view this as moving from debate to dialogue, which we shall be exploring in Chapter 49, 'Debate and dialogue'. In terms of the Thomas-Kilmann conflict handling framework that we looked at in the previous chapter, a learning conversation is about collaborating rather than competing.

If you are preparing to have a difficult or fierce conversation, here are three useful questions to consider in advance:

1. What do I want for myself?
2. What do I want for the other person?
3. What do I want for the relationship?

A common issue in coaching is that the client finds it difficult to be assertive – perhaps in general, or perhaps in specific relationships. Helping the client to find their voice, and to develop the skills and confidence to say clearly what they think or want, can be a real challenge.

An approach I sometimes take when a client finds it difficult to be assertive in some situations is to ask them if there are other situations when they feel able to speak up confidently. I offer the idea that each of us has different selves. For example, I think and act differently when I'm coaching than I do when I'm playing five-a-side football. There's *Bob the coach* and *Bob the ageing footballer*! I invite the client to explore how they are in their different situations – how they think, feel, behave and speak. I sometimes ask them to sit in different chairs as they talk through their different selves. And then I ask them to give a name to each of their selves, one that somehow captures the essence of their two characters – let's say they choose *Anxious Alex* and *Artistic Alex*. It's important that they choose the names, not me. And we then explore how they can bring out, in this case, Artistic Alex, when they are in the situations where they find it difficult to speak up. This may lead them to trying things out in practice before our next session, making some notes on how they fared. We can then review how they got on – in the spirit of learning, not judging.

Voicing is also a useful conversational skill for a coach. There may be times when you wish to share your thinking or your opinion with the client, perhaps moving towards the directive end of the spectrum. Or, you may wish to challenge the client in some way. Or, you may wish to address issues that have arisen in the relationship between you and the client. If you do share your views, it's important to be able to voice these clearly and also succinctly. Lengthy statements from the coach take the focus away from the client and their issues.

In Chapter 40 we'll look at mediation. Coaching skills – listening, questioning and playing back – are an invaluable foundation for a mediator. There are also times in mediation when a mediator has to speak assertively in order to manage the conversation. For example, one party may be more powerful or simply more articulate than the other. The mediator may have to speak up in order to ensure that both parties have the opportunity to express their views. Voicing is a key part of the mediator's skill set.

**VIDEO**

In this four-minute video Susan Scott talks about the importance for individuals and organisations in having the conversations that really matter: www.youtube.com/watch?v=wQPCM40fb-s

## References

Scott, S (2002) *Fierce Conversations: Achieving Success in Work and in Life, One Conversation at a Time*. London: Piatkus.

Stone, D, Patton, B and Heen, S (1999) *Difficult Conversations: How to Discuss What Matters Most*. New York: Viking Penguin.

# Chapter 23: W

## WRITING

---

Coaching generally takes place through conversations in which the coach asks the client questions to help them explore their situation and to consider possible actions to address the challenges they're facing. There are other things that the coach can do within a session. For example, they might offer a model or framework Or they might help the client to work through the results of a psychometric test that they've completed, or take them through 360-degree feedback. In this chapter we look at the use of writing within a coaching session, and also as a follow-up activity.

There are a number of situations within a coaching conversation when I'm prompted to ask the client to do some writing. One is when I've asked the client to make some kind of list – maybe to note down their options or to capture the pros and cons of a possible action. I do sometimes make a list myself, perhaps to play this back to the client or maybe just to help me make some notes that I may refer back to later in the session. But, if the client is producing a list, my preference is to ask them to write it.

Another prompt to ask the client to write is when I want, in a sense, to slow the conversation down to invite the client to think carefully about something. Asking them to capture their thoughts in writing means that they take longer to respond than if I'd simply asked an equivalent question. I generally don't want them to speak as they write, but rather to share with me their reflections once they've completed the task. Writing things down also gives them a record of their thoughts that they may refer to later.

A particular form of writing that I occasionally use is to ask the client to write a letter. As an illustration, let's suppose that a client is exploring their future career direction. I may ask them to pick a point in the future and imagine that their career is working out really well. I also ask them to choose someone who is – or was – significant to them. I invite them to write a letter from this future point to this person, telling them what they've done between today and the time in the future that they selected. Thus the letter is about the future, not past achievements. I ask them to write it as a letter, not in bullet points – I think this helps to free up their thinking. I also tell them before they start writing that it's up to them how much of the letter they share with me when they've finished. That allows them to explore their thoughts and feelings about matters which they don't necessarily wish to share. If this is a coaching session in my office, I may leave the client to do this and go off to make them a tea or coffee. When they've finished writing, I ask them to read whatever they wish to share, and we then explore this in conversation. One question I often ask as we near the close is, 'What surprises you about what you've written?'

A further way to use writing in coaching is to invite the client to write between sessions. For example, you may have agreed that it would be useful for the client to try out some new ways of thinking and behaving – let's say, to speak up more assertively in meetings. They can capture notes after meetings on what they did well and less well. They might also scale their performance from one to ten, where ten means they performed excellently. At the next session, we can review together their notes on how they got on – in the spirit of helping them to learn further, not to judge or criticise.

Another way to use writing to reflect upon and learn from you experience is to keep a journal. We considered this in the chapter on the Kolb learning cycle. This might be of value to you yourself as a coach reflecting on your practice, or to some of your clients. A journal isn't the same as a diary – you don't have to write every day. Rather, it's a place where you can capture your thoughts and feelings about meaningful events. It's up to the individual to choose the format for doing this. Some people write in a notebook, while others capture their reflections on a computer or phone. Some include poems or quotes or photographs or their own drawings. The key points are that the format is both simple to use and appealing for the writer. Looking back at a journal over time may reveal patterns, and indicate how things have changed, or perhaps stagnated. In their book *Reflective Writing in Counselling and Psychotherapy*, Jeannie Wright and Gillie Bolton say that:

> *Journal writing has the power to help people understand themselves, each other, their relationships with each other and their world better. It draws on the imagination and deep memory as well as logical cognitive thought.*
>
> (Wright and Bolton, 2012)

I once collaborated with Jeannie Wright when she was in charge of counselling programmes at the University of Warwick's Centre for Lifelong Learning to set up an internal scheme within the university called Coaching Through Reflective Writing. I coached staff who wished to be coached in this way over a period of months. The client would email me their thoughts as and when they wished to, and I would respond to them by email. We set each coaching relationship up with an initial face-to-face meeting. And we ensured that all correspondence was confidential and handled securely.

In my normal day-to-day practice as a coach or supervisor, I invite clients to email me whenever they wish to ask a quick question, or check something out, or want to arrange a conversation before our next scheduled session. I see these emails as complementing, but not as a substitute for, our coaching conversations.

**REFLECTIVE TASK**

This exercise invites you to try out the idea of writing a letter to a significant other.

- Identify an area of your coaching practice, or your work, or in your life outside work where you would like to operate differently and more effectively than you currently do.
- Choose someone who is – or was – significant to you and who would be very interested in your progress in this area.
- Choose an appropriate point in the future. Imagine that things have worked out well and that you are indeed operating more effectively in this area.
- Write a letter dated from this future point to this person, telling them how you're performing and what you did between today and this future time to enhance your effectiveness. You might also share how you're thinking and feeling at this future point. (I encourage you to write this as if it were a letter to this person who matters to you, not as a set of bullet points or a project report.)

The letter may be a useful resource for you to identify goals and action steps and monitoring points in regard to the issue you chose.

- One final question: What surprises you about what you wrote?

## Reference

Wright, J and Bolton, G (2012) *Reflective Writing in Counselling and Psychotherapy.* London: Sage.

# Chapter 24: X

## EXTRAVERTS AND INTROVERTS

I don't have anything to say about X-rays or xylophones or the ancient Greek king Xerxes. And I don't watch *The X Factor* on TV. So, I'm going to cheat for the letter X. In this chapter I look at the notion of Extraverts and Introverts.

The Myers-Briggs Type Indicator, or MBTI, is the most widely used personality profile in the world. It was developed originally by a mother and daughter, Katharine Briggs and Isabel Briggs Myers. It is a self-report instrument constructed from how you answer a series of questions on yourself. It's based on the psychological theories of Carl Jung, a contemporary of Sigmund Freud. While some coaches will explore a client's full MBTI profile in coaching them, it's also possible simply to consider each of the four dimensions that make up the profile. Although I'm trained to use the full MBTI, in practice I generally use one of the dimensions as a model to help a client to make sense of and, if they choose to, modify their behaviour.

MBTI is based on *types* rather than *traits* – it considers that each of us, for example, is naturally either an Extravert or an Introvert. It doesn't view this dimension as lying along a bell-shaped normal distribution. To use an analogy, you are born either right-handed or left-handed, you can't be naturally ambidextrous. Experiences, such as family upbringing, education or the jobs that you do, may overlay your natural preference, and so influence how you behave. But, according to Myers and Briggs, your underlying personality type doesn't change.

There are four dimensions in the MBTI, and each is given a letter, which leads to a four-letter summary of each personality type (Table 24.1).

**Table 24.1 Dimensions of the Myers-Briggs Type Indicator**

| | |
|---|---|
| **Extraversion (E)** People who prefer Extraversion like to focus on the outer world of people and activity. | **Introversion (I)** People who prefer Introversion like to focus on their own inner world of ideas and experiences. |
| **Sensing (S)** People who prefer Sensing like to take in information that is real and tangible – what is actually happening. | **Intuition (N)** People who prefer Intuition like to take in information by seeing the big picture, focusing on the relationships and connections between facts. |
| **Thinking (T)** People who prefer to use Thinking in decision-making like to look at the logical consequences of a choice or action. | **Feeling (F)** People who prefer to use Feeling in decision-making like to consider what is important to them and to others involved. |
| **Judging (J)** People who use their Judging process in the outer world like to live in a planned, orderly way, seeking to regulate and manage their lives. | **Perceiving (P)** People who prefer to use their Perceiving process in the outer world like to live in a flexible, spontaneous way, seeking to experience and understand life, rather than control it. |

My own MBTI profile is INTP. I actually disagree with the view that each dimension is a type rather than a trait. I know that I have a very clear preference for both I and N, but I believe I'm close to the middle on the final two dimensions. The website of the Myers and Briggs Foundation has this summary description of a typical INTP. I recognise myself in the description!

> *Seek to develop logical explanations for everything that interests them. Theoretical and abstract, interested more in ideas than in social interaction. Quiet, contained, flexible, and adaptable. Have unusual ability to focus in depth to solve problems in their area of interest. Sceptical, sometimes critical, always analytical.*
>
> (Myers and Briggs Foundation, 2022a)

There are a number of amusing summaries or caricatures of the 16 MBTI types. One of these lists short prayers for each type. My own MBTI prayer, which again reflects me well, reads:

> *Lord, help me be less independent, but let me do it my way.*
>
> (Georgetown Faculty, nd)

The dimension that I draw upon most often in coaching is the Extravert–Introvert dimension. Here are two descriptions from the Myers and Briggs Foundation website.

*Extravert*

> *I like getting my energy from active involvement in events and having a lot of different activities. I'm excited when I'm around people and I like to energize other people. I like moving into action and making things happen. I generally feel at home in the world. I often understand a problem better when I can talk out loud about it and hear what others have to say.*

*Introvert*

> *I like getting my energy from dealing with the ideas, pictures, memories, and reactions that are inside my head, in my inner world. I often prefer doing things alone or with one or two people I feel comfortable with. I take time to reflect so that I have a clear idea of what I'll be doing when I decide*

*to act. Ideas are almost solid things for me. Sometimes I like the idea of something better than the real thing.*
(Myers and Briggs Foundation, 2022b)

One way of caricaturing the difference between Extraverts and Introverts is that Extraverts speak first and then maybe think, while Introverts think first and then maybe speak. I recall one manager who had a very clear preference for Extraversion express his view that *'If you have nothing to say, it's important to say it eloquently!'*

I find that I usually refer to this aspect of personality much more with Introverts than Extraverts. The former are more likely to find it difficult to speak up and be heard in meetings. In her book *Quiet: The Power of Introverts in a World That Can't Stop Talking*, Susan Cain (2012) explores how Western culture values Extraversion much more than Introversion.

In a coaching session with someone who, like me, has a strong Introvert preference, I may emphasise that, while it's not possible to change your personality, you can modify your behaviour. I sometimes (moving towards the directive end of the spectrum) share some of the tips below that I myself find helpful.

- In some meetings where I want to be seen as an active participant, I will say something early in the meeting – this makes it easier for me to make other contributions later.
- I often find it easier to ask a question or to offer a summary, rather than to state what I think. These can be helpful behaviours in meetings.
- I use what I call *signposting*, where I begin a contribution by saying something like, *'I have a couple of points that I want to make.'*
- Since I take time to process my thoughts, I sometimes give myself permission to speak before I've fully worked out my view by saying something like, *'Let me think out loud for a moment.'*

As these examples illustrate, awareness of your own preference is helpful in self-management.

Moreover, awareness of the preferences of both yourself and others is valuable in managing relationships. For example, a line manager with an Extravert preference may deliberately hold back in meetings and consciously invite people with an Introvert preference to share their views. Or they might give Introverts time to think – for instance, by letting them know in advance of a meeting areas where they'd like to hear from them.

**VIDEO**

This six-minute animated video goes into more depth in discussing Extraverts and Introverts. Interestingly, it suggests that the dimension is a trait rather than a type, and it describes people in the middle as Ambiverts. It also considers how a teacher or leader can develop individuals with differing preferences: www.youtube.com/watch?v= acg6HivAu5E

## References

Cain, S. (2012) *Quiet: The Power of Introverts in a World That Can't Stop Talking*. New York: Random House.

Georgetown Faculty (nd) MBTI-Types Prayers. [online] Available at: https://faculty.georgetown.edu/jod/texts/mbprayers.html (accessed 26 September 2022).

Myers and Briggs Foundation (2022a) The 16 MBTI Types. [online] Available at: www.myersbriggs.org/my-mbti-personality-type/mbti-basics/the-16-mbti-types.htm (accessed 26 September 2022).

Myers and Briggs Foundation (2022b) Extraversion or Intraversion. [online] Available at: www.myersbriggs.org/my-mbti-personality-type/mbti-basics/extraversion-or-introversion.htm (accessed 26 September 2022).

# Chapter 25: Y

## THEORY Y AND THEORY X

In his book *The Human Side of Enterprise*, Douglas McGregor (1960) discussed two styles of management – *Theory X* (authoritarian) and *Theory Y* (participative). In this chapter we look at these two perspectives, and consider several other views on what motivates people.

In Chapter 41, 'Coaching as a line manager', we will set out the idea of a coaching dance in which a manager moves skilfully between the directive end of the spectrum, where they tell people what to do, and the non-directive end, where they ask questions to tap into the ideas and creativity of their staff. Part of the skill lies in knowing when to *Tell* and when to *Ask*. Many managers operate exclusively from the *Tell* position, with a *Command and Control* style of management.

A Theory X view of people assumes that they are inherently lazy, dislike work and seek to avoid responsibility. If this is your underlying mental model, you are unlikely to trust your staff. Managing people from this perspective is indeed about Command and Control. If incentives and punishments are available to you, you are likely to use a mix of carrot and stick to ensure compliance with your instructions or orders. This may reflect a wider organisational culture where there are multiple levels in the hierarchy, with central control, tight objectives and little delegation of authority.

In contrast, a Theory Y perspective assumes that people enjoy work and are talented, creative and able to motivate themselves.

As a manager, if this is how you view your people, then your assumption is that they want to do a good job, and that this desire in itself is motivating. Hence you are likely to communicate openly, share decision-making and generate a climate of trust. A coaching approach sits well within a Theory Y mental model of the world.

In his book *The Motivation to Work*, Frederick Herzberg (1959) suggested on the basis of his survey of 200 engineers and accountants that people at work have two sets of needs. First, there are basic needs such as remuneration, working conditions and security. These are *hygiene factors* – their presence doesn't motivate but their absence can demotivate. As an illustration, having a car park space near the office is convenient, but it won't motivate you. But if management take away your car park space, it's likely to demotivate you! Hygiene factors are found in the surroundings of a job – in company policies, working conditions and remuneration.

Second, there are factors such as achievement, meaningful contribution, recognition, responsibility, advancement and personal growth that are genuinely motivating for people. *Motivating factors* are within the actual job itself. Herzberg coined the term *job enrichment*, which is about including motivating factors in the design of jobs.

It's interesting to consider Herzberg's framework alongside McGregor's. A Theory X view of employees would suggest that raising pay or improving working conditions will motivate staff. The question of whether pay is a motivator or a hygiene factor is the cause of some debate. In some contexts, perhaps in a sales environment, paying bonuses based on results may be a strong motivator of performance. From a Theory Y view, enhancing hygiene factors won't motivate people in anything but the very short term. I recall a time many years ago when a close colleague was feeling very disgruntled at work. Our boss gave him a bonus, which uplifted my friend's mood but only for a day or two. It wasn't a wise investment.

Another well-known model of motivation is Abraham Maslow's hierarchy of needs which he described his book *Motivation and Personality* (1954). The five levels in the hierarchy, shown in Figure 25.1, are the following.

1. *Self-actualisation* – personal growth and fulfilment.
2. *Esteem* – achievement, status, respect of others, self-esteem.
3. *Belonging* – love, friendship, family.
4. *Safety needs* – health, security, employment, etc.
5. *Physiological needs* – air, food and water, shelter, sleep, etc.

**Figure 25.1  Maslow's hierarchy of needs**

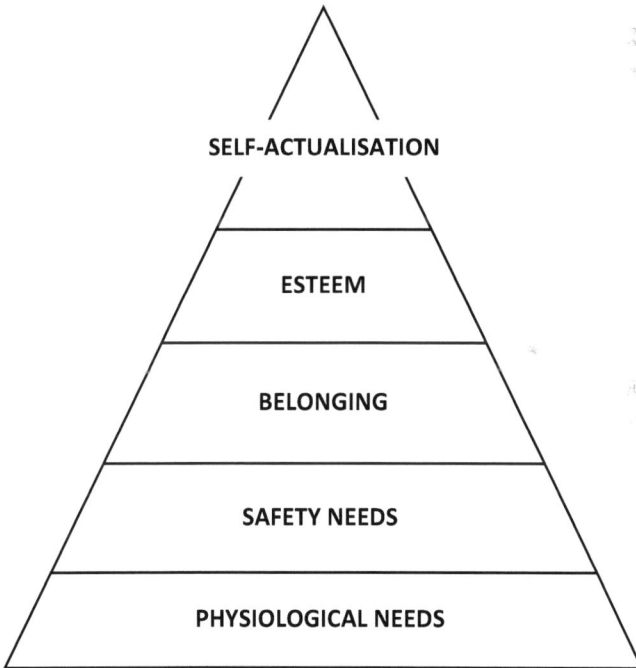

SELF-ACTUALISATION

ESTEEM

BELONGING

SAFETY NEEDS

PHYSIOLOGICAL NEEDS

When physiological or safety needs at the lower levels are unmet, then an individual will focus their efforts on satisfying these needs. Only when their lower levels are satisfied will a person seek to satisfy their higher needs for belonging, esteem and self-actualisation. At times of significant change – for example, when someone's job and livelihood are at risk – people are likely to slip down the hierarchy of needs and be more concerned about putting food on the table and paying the mortgage than about their status or personal development.

In his book *The Achieving Society*, David McClelland (1961) built on Maslow's ideas to explore three motivators that he reckons we all have, but in varying degrees. Depending on our culture and experiences, each of us has one of the three motivators as our dominant driver.

1. Someone with a need for *Power* is motivated by having a position of power or control.
2. Someone with a need for *Achievement* is motivated by success or achieving objectives.
3. Someone with a need for *Affiliation* is motivated by working in a collaborative environment or group.

It's interesting that these four theories of motivation were first published in the 1950s or early 1960s. In a 2008 article called 'Managing with the Brain in Mind', David Rock drew on ideas from the then emerging field of neuroscience to set out a framework of five factors that affect the extent to which people feel engaged at work. It is based on the idea that our brains are organised to minimise threat and maximise reward, and is known by the mnemonic SCARF.

- **S**tatus
- **C**ertainty
- **A**utonomy
- **R**elatedness
- **F**airness

We discuss the SCARF model in more detail in Chapter 39, 'Neuroscience, the SCARF model and the Chimp Paradox'.

**REFLECTIVE TASK**

Here are some questions inviting you to reflect upon what motivates you yourself and on what you believe motivates others.

- To what extent do you take a Theory X or Theory Y view of the people that you work with or collaborate with?
- For you personally, to what extent is pay and remuneration a hygiene factor or a genuine motivator?
- In terms of Maslow's hierarchy of needs, what needs are you currently seeking to satisfy in your work and more generally in your life?
- In a work context, what would you say is your dominant driver – power, achievement or affiliation?

## References

Herzberg, F (1959) *The Motivation to Work*. New York: Wiley.

Maslow, A (1954) *Motivation and Personality*. New York: Harper.

McClelland, D (1961) *The Achieving Society*. Princeton: Van Nostrand.

McGregor, D (1960) *The Human Side of Enterprise*. New York: McGraw-Hill.

Rock, D (2008) Managing with the Brain in Mind. *NeuroLeadership Journal*, 1(1): 1–9.

# Chapter 26: Z

## ZOOM

---

I've written this book entirely in my study at home. I've become used to working a lot of the time from home since the start of lockdown in the spring of 2020. As I noted in Chapter 24, 'Extraverts and Introverts', I'm an Introvert, and working from home has suited me. I suspect that, to generalise, Introverts have found this easier than Extraverts. I also love not having to drive to and from work each day. However, I'm keen that our students have as much face-to-face contact as possible. Over the Easter term 2022, I did all of my teaching in person, apart from one session when I had to isolate because I had Covid.

If you had asked me before the start of the pandemic about the relative merits of coaching face-to-face and coaching via telephone or Skype, I would have said that the former was much better. I did almost all of my coaching face-to-face, usually in my office at Warwick Business School. I did do the occasional session remotely, and I remember that I much preferred phone to Skype. This was partly because I could take notes to keep track of the conversation on the phone without distracting the client.

Now, after two years of coaching almost exclusively via Zoom or MS Teams, I've changed my view. I find that coaching and also supervision sessions work very well remotely. Yes, sometimes there are connection problems, and occasionally sound quality isn't great. I've learnt to make a note of the other person's phone number in case the connection goes down. But I've been able to maintain or, with new clients, develop some great coaching or supervision relationships.

I've also conducted a number of mediations remotely. I still think there's a big advantage in the two participants in mediation sitting down in a room together to exchange their views, but it has worked surprisingly well via Zoom or Teams.

One of the main practical advantages in conversing remotely is that there's no need for either participant to travel. For example, I have a client in Oxford. We started coaching a few months before the first lockdown, and this laid a great foundation for our work together. However, travelling to and from there from my home in Stratford-upon-Avon for a 90-minute coaching session took up three-quarters of a day. Since the first lockdown, all of our sessions have been via Teams. Now I can arrange my calendar to accommodate many more things in a day than I possibly could if I had to move between venues. I have a friend who has a supervisee in Kuwait and another in Taiwan – this simply wouldn't work if sessions were face-to-face.

One of my roles at Warwick Business School is that I'm a senior tutor for half of our final year undergraduates. All of our students have a personal tutor. It's usually the more serious issues that get raised with a senior tutor. My coaching experience is very helpful in my conversations with students. Over the past two years, these conversations have been almost exclusively via Teams. Again, there are practical, time-saving advantages for both of us, particularly for a student living off campus who might otherwise have had to take a bus to and from the university, perhaps just for one 20- or 30-minute conversation.

Universities have had to make large adjustments to teaching arrangements over the past couple of years. Initially, all lectures, seminars and exams at Warwick moved online. We've been working back towards a face-to-face model. I don't think we'll ever get back fully to what we had before, but a new hybrid model that combines the best of both remote and face-to-face sessions may well be better than what we had before the pandemic struck. For instance, while some lecturers are inspirational, many 50-minute lectures to several hundred students have been delivered just as well through a recording. This has the added advantages that students can watch the lecture at a time that suits them and can rewatch sections that they find particularly difficult or interesting.

Most meetings have also moved online. Again, I find it much easier to fit these into my calendar. A disadvantage is that informal conversations before or after a meeting generally don't take place. This might affect the quality of working relationships. One other advantage in attending some larger meetings remotely is that it's not disruptive to switch off your camera and your microphone in order to get on with other work when topics that you're not interested in are being discussed. As we noted in the chapter on listening, sometimes it's okay not to listen!

In response to the lockdown and the move to remote working, I collaborated with three colleagues from the university's Wellbeing Services team to design and deliver a series of webinars to help managers in the university explore how to build resilience and provide effective coping mechanisms, both for themselves and for their staff. We delivered each session via MS Teams. I now feel that I know these three colleagues well and that we have a sound working relationship, even though I've never met any of them in person.

You might be wondering why I've called this chapter 'Zoom' rather than 'MS Teams'. Different organisations favoured different systems. The University of Warwick opted for Teams rather than Zoom. So, although I have taken part in Zoom meetings arranged externally, most of my remote teaching, coaching, supervision and mediation sessions have been via MS Teams. But I was struggling to find a topic beginning with Z!

**READING**

In 2021 I supported a colleague, Naomi de la Tour, who led a learning circle of staff and students at the University of Warwick on the topic of 'Learning from the Crisis'. We used a framework developed by Ian Burbidge, Head of Innovation and Change at the Royal Society of Arts (RSA), to explore which activities to prioritise in the light of our experience of adjusting to the pandemic, lockdown and remote working.

In our discussions we sought to identify:

- Activities that we had stopped doing and which we don't need to restart. *(Let go)*
- Activities that we had stopped doing but which we now need to restart. *(Restart)*
- Activities which we had started in response to the crisis but which we can now drop. *(End)*
- Activities which we had started in response to the crisis and which we should continue to do. *(Amplify)*

Having coaching or supervision sessions via Teams or Zoom certainly falls into the final category for me!

You can read more about the RSA framework in this blog post by Ian Burbidge: www.thersa.org/blog/2020/04/change-covid19-response

You might find it useful to apply the framework to reflect upon what you or your organisation have learnt from your experiences during the Covid crisis.

And back again ...

# Chapter 27: Z

## ZONE OF PROXIMAL DEVELOPMENT

The Soviet psychologist Lev Vygotsky created the concept of the *Zone of Proximal Development* (ZPD) as a key idea in the development of children. The Zone of Proximal Development is the space between what a learner can do on their own without assistance and what they cannot yet do. It is the area where they can do things with guidance or support from another, or in collaboration with more capable peers, or perhaps with help from online resources (Figure 27.1).

**Figure 27.1  The Zone of Proximal Development**

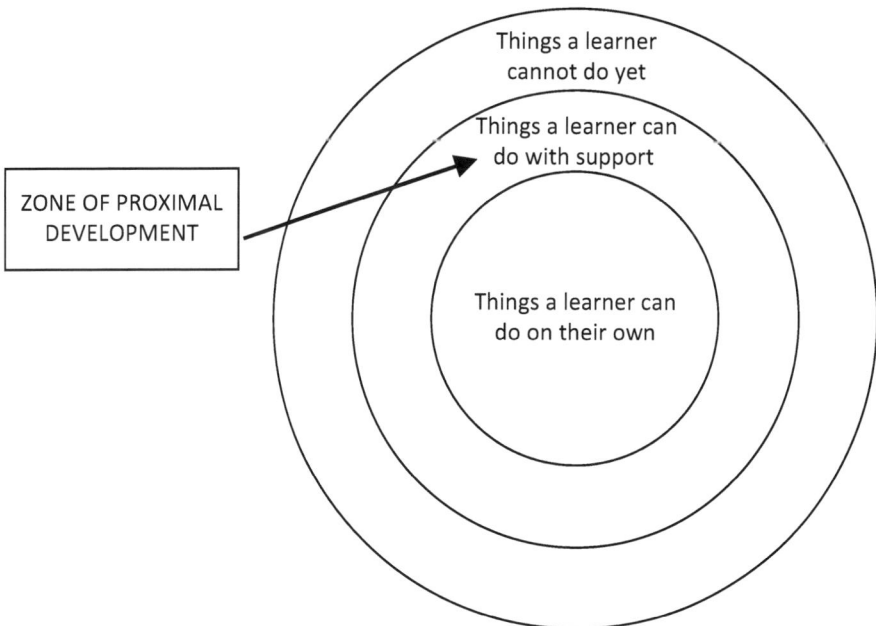

ZONE OF PROXIMAL DEVELOPMENT

Things a learner cannot do yet

Things a learner can do with support

Things a learner can do on their own

One of my colleagues at the University of Warwick, Sue Johnston-Wilder, draws on this idea in her work on *maths anxiety*. For many people the barrier to learning maths is emotional rather than cognitive. Maths anxiety affects people of all ages and across the globe. It often arises from poor and distressing experiences in a classroom when a student is labelled as 'thick' or lazy or disruptive because they aren't able to grasp what a maths teacher is trying to impart. Ignoring, humiliating or isolating a student – and all of these do happen – causes emotional harm. Faced with a new idea in maths or statistics, or perhaps something simply involving numbers, the student becomes anxious or panics, leading to a flight, fight or freeze response.

Sue renames the three zones the green or comfort zone, the amber or growth zone, and the red or anxiety zone. She uses a coaching approach with students to help them, first, to recognise which zone they're in at any point and, second, to do something useful in response. You might regard this as raising awareness and encouraging responsibility. So, a student might ask a question or say they don't understand. Speaking up in a maths class may be difficult for a student with maths anxiety to do. Alternatively, they might do a breathing or mindfulness exercise to calm themselves down. Ideas such as these help a student to develop what Sue calls their *mathematical resilience*.

She also uses a coaching approach with teachers to help them reframe what is happening when students don't understand maths ideas. If a student is panicking, then repeating something, speaking louder or just moving on with the lesson isn't going to help them. A useful idea to help someone in the amber zone – that is, the Zone of Proximal Development – is the notion of *scaffolding*.

On a construction site, scaffolding helps builders to work at greater heights. In education, scaffolding helps students to learn new things. The teacher will make an initial assessment of what a student understands. They then offer appropriate support, such as breaking up concepts, sharing new information or demonstrating how to solve a problem. As the student begins to grasp things, the teacher gradually steps back and lets them practise on their own. Hence scaffolding supports the student as they move through the Zone of Proximal Development. It enables a student to solve a problem or achieve a goal that they couldn't have done on their own. It takes a student from what they cannot do through what they can do with assistance to what they can do unaided. Back on the construction site, the scaffolding is removed when the building is completed.

As an illustration, imagine the process of learning to drive a car. Most people don't simply get in a car for the first time and drive off. They work with some form of driving instructor who initially provides a lot of support and guidance, taking the learner on quiet roads without much traffic. As the learner becomes more capable – and more confident – the instructor takes them on busier roads and offers much less instruction. And one day the learner passes their driving test and is qualified to drive on their own, unaided. They will then, without the aid of an instructor, continue to improve their skills as they gain experience of driving on even more challenging roads and in different traffic conditions.

I draw on the ideas of the ZPD and of scaffolding in helping people learn how to coach. As an illustration, I run a Certificate in Coaching Practice for undergraduate students at the University of Warwick. It's based on five two-hour workshops spread over a term. In the first sessions I introduce foundational ideas, such as listening, questioning and the GROW model. Students practise their skills in short coaching sessions with each other. I later introduce more advanced ideas – for example, practical and ethical matters, the inner game and solution-focused coaching. Each student goes on to work with a practice client for three or four sessions. They complete a 1,000-word reflective essay to gain the Certificate. My intention is to enable them over the course of several months to build their coaching skills and to develop confidence in using these in purposeful conversations.

You can also apply the ideas when working with a coaching client. If the issue they face lies within their comfort zone, then they can tackle it on their own, although you may need to encourage them to address it. It is the issues that lie within the client's ZPD that require your support, encouragement and perhaps appropriate challenge. One way of framing the role of the coach is as someone who provides suitable scaffolding to enable the client to learn how to address their challenges effectively – initially with the support of the coach and later without their support.

As an illustration, imagine a client whose challenge is that they find it hard to speak up in certain meetings. Telling them not to be a wimp and *'just get on and do it'* isn't likely to be helpful. Offering understanding and acceptance, sharing some ideas, helping them to rehearse during the session, agreeing tasks that they'll work on between sessions, asking them to make notes on their experience, and reviewing progress at the next session – these are all pieces of scaffolding to help the client learn how to speak up in meetings. And they might go on to draw on their learning to increase their confidence and effectiveness in other, perhaps even more challenging, contexts.

You can also view the supervision process as a way of helping a coach to address challenges in their coaching practice that sit within their Zone of Proximal Development.

**READING**

You can read more about the Zone of Proximal Development and scaffolding in this article: www.verywellmind.com/what-is-the-zone-of-proximal-development-2796034

# Chapter 28: Y

## YOUR OWN COACHING PRACTICE OR BUSINESS

For a number of years I had the pleasure of running a Certificate in Coaching at the University of Warwick's Centre for Lifelong Learning. The participants were generally mature students from a variety of backgrounds. Some of them wanted to develop their coaching skills for use in their job as a manager, social worker, HR professional or academic. And for others the motivation was because they were interested in becoming a coach. Some of these were women who had interrupted their first career to have a family, and they wanted to explore if becoming a coach would be a good way for them personally to return to the world of work.

Coaching isn't a regulated profession. Anyone can call themself a coach. But to become a coach who is actively engaged with clients isn't easy. Many of the students on the Certificate didn't go on to become an active coach, while others have built successful coaching businesses.

My own journey to becoming a coach wasn't planned in advance but emerged over time. In the late 1990s I was working in management development in the gas pipeline company Transco. Almost by accident, I went on the first coaching programme offered by the School of Coaching. Run by Myles Downey and Jane Meyler, it gave me a superb foundation in coaching skills, complementing well my background as a facilitator of experiential management development. I set up a programme to help Transco managers develop their coaching skills, which gave me the privilege of working alongside and learning from John Whitmore, David Whitaker, David Hemery and Sue Slocombe. I left Transco to join the University of Warwick in an internal Learning and Development role at the start of 2005. I set up a leadership programme for Warwick academics, administrators and commercial managers. This consisted of a mix of workshops, 360-degree feedback and coaching sessions – the latter gave me lots of opportunity to practise and enhance my coaching skills. So, my own journey to become a coach was as an internal coach within two organisations. This had the advantage that I didn't need to develop a commercial business. Being able to coach well and being able to market coaching services effectively are two very different skills!

If you are at or near the start of your coaching journey, one way of taking this forward is to work as an internal coach within an organisation. It will be easier to do this within your current organisation than to join another organisation as a relatively inexperienced coach. You might explore with your Human Resources or Learning and Development teams if there are opportunities to coach other members of staff. The University of Warwick, for example, has a scheme where staff can volunteer to be trained as and to work internally as a coach. Or, it might be that your organisation has a mentoring scheme where you can grow your experience in managing purposeful conversations that support the development of another.

If you do have a good amount of coaching experience, a second option may be to join a firm that specialises in offering coaching commercially. Some of these are at the high end of the market and recruit people who have worked at board level in FTSE 100 companies or were successful Olympic athletes. But others, who may also offer a range of learning and development or human resource services alongside their coaching services, recruit from a wider range of people.

A third option is to set yourself up as an independent coach, running your own coaching company. As I noted earlier, this requires business development skills alongside coaching skills. Being able to network well is a great help here. If you've just left an organisation, there may be useful contacts there who can offer you work as a coach. In building a business as a coach, word-of-mouth referral can be invaluable.

A fourth option is to make a living through a portfolio of activities, with coaching as one element. Some people continue working part time in the field they were employed in, perhaps expanding their coaching practice over time. An advantage of having coaching as one part of a mixed portfolio is that it gives you a break from what you might experience as the intensity of coaching conversations, with an opportunity to recharge your batteries by doing something different.

In pursuing the third or fourth options, it can be useful to become an associate of one or more coaching or other organisations. This has the advantage that you yourself don't have to do the marketing to find the work, although some associates are also involved in helping to win business for their partners. A downside of being an associate is that you get paid a fraction of the fee, with the associate firm keeping the remainder – which strikes me as a fair arrangement. And, as you grow your coaching business, you yourself might draw on others as associates to support you if, for example, you win a large piece of work or if the need is for a specialised service that you yourself don't offer. Some coaches utilise associates to free themself up to do the work that is most interesting and rewarding for them. I know several people who were very successful career coaches whose interests have taken them away from this into leadership or team coaching. If you are developing your own business, you might also think about paying other people to provide accounting, secretarial, marketing or IT services to free yourself to concentrate on your work as a coach.

In Chapter 26, 'Zoom', we discussed how over the past few years much coaching work has moved to online rather than face-to-face conversations. This offers practical advantages if you are looking to start or expand your coaching business. Two key factors are that you don't need to find premises to conduct face-to-face sessions and there is far less need for you or your clients to travel to meet one another.

If you are thinking of developing your own coaching work commercially, I recommend a book by Jenny Rogers (2017) called *Building a Coaching Business*. Drawing on her considerable experience, she takes the reader through ten steps to creating a successful and profitable coaching practice.

In Chapter 19, 'Supervision', we explored the value of working with a supervisor to reflect upon and enhance your coaching. Some of my own supervisees discuss business development matters in our sessions. Others, alongside their supervision with me, also work with a business development mentor who can offer specialised support and guidance on the commercial and organisational aspects of growing a coaching business.

Wherever you are on your coaching journey, I wish you well for the next steps on your adventure.

**READING**

The link below is a preview of the second edition of Jenny Rogers' book. Each chapter explores one of her ten steps that will help establish a thriving coaching business: www.google.co.uk/books/edition/EBOOK_Building_a_Coaching_Business_Ten_s/VsovEAAAQBAJ?hl=en&gbpv=1&printsec=frontcover

## Reference

Rogers, J (2017) *Building a Coaching Business: Ten Steps to Success* (2nd edition). Maidenhead: Open University Press.

# Chapter 29: X

## EXPLORING METAPHORS

As with the other chapter for the letter X, 'Extraverts and Introverts', I'm cheating with this chapter, 'Exploring metaphors'. *Xenophobia* didn't seem an appropriate topic.

In their classic book on the subject, *Metaphors We Live By*, George Lakoff and Mark Johnson (1980) explain how metaphor is much more than a matter of language. Not only do we speak in metaphors, each of us also thinks in terms of metaphors. And how we think shapes how we act. In another classic book, *Images of Organization*, where he explores eight metaphors that underpin how we view organisations, Gareth Morgan emphasises the fundamental importance of metaphor:

> *The use of metaphor implies a way of thinking and a way of seeing that pervade how we understand our world generally.*
>
> (Morgan, 1996)

A metaphor is capable of capturing vividly a great deal of abstract and intangible information in a concise and memorable package.

All metaphors are partial and, moreover, are neither true nor false. The value of a metaphor depends on the richness of the insights it generates. These points are important when we consider the use of metaphor within coaching.

I find that there are times when a coaching client spontaneously uses an especially striking metaphor. As an illustration, a client who was struggling in various ways with challenges at work said to me, '*I feel like I'm alone in a vast ocean.*' Later in the conversation, after we'd explored her situation and possible options, she said, '*I'm still adrift, but I can see the shoreline.*' There was a power and meaning in her choice of words.

When a client shares a vivid metaphor, it's useful to encourage them to explore it further. In my illustration, I might have said, '*Tell me more about feeling alone in a vast ocean.*' Or I might have simply repeated her metaphor '*vast ocean?*' with an inquisitive tone. As they explore – or perhaps play with – their metaphor, new insights may emerge for the client, and these may in turn lead to possible actions.

In her book *Time to Think,* Nancy Kline emphasises the importance of working with the client's own words:

> *The best wording is the Thinker's own: their mind has specifically chosen and uttered those exact words for a reason. Those words mean something to the Thinker. They come from somewhere and are rich with the Thinker's history, culture, experience and any number of associations in the Thinker's life.*
>
> (Kline, 1999)

There is an approach called *Clean Language*, which is based on asking some very specific questions that invite a client to explore deeply their metaphors, using the exact words of the client. Clean Language practitioners believe that helping a client to explore their metaphors and symbols can enable them to address issues at a deeper level than the conscious mind can reach. In their book *Metaphors in Mind*, which has the subtitle *Transformation through Symbolic Modelling*, James Lawley and Penny Tompkins write:

> *We define Symbolic Modelling as a process, which uses Clean Language to facilitate people's discovery of how their metaphors express their way of being in the world.*
>
> (Lawley and Tompkins, 2000)

There are 12 basic Clean Language questions. I illustrate three of these, which are known as the *Name and Address questions*, using my previous example:

- (And) what kind of vast ocean (is that vast ocean)?
- (And) is there anything else about vast ocean?
- (And) where is vast ocean?

If the idea appeals to you and you'd like to find out more about using Clean Language in coaching, you might look at the book *Clean Language: Revealing Metaphors and Opening Minds* by Wendy Sullivan and Judy Rees (2008).

In my own practice, I see the value in working with the exact words of a client, and I find it useful to invite a client to explore their metaphors. However, I'm not aiming to work with them at a subconscious level, as Clean Language practitioners may do. I think this is beyond the boundaries of my competence, and also outside the unspoken contract that we have for our work together.

Another way in which I sometimes work with metaphor in a coaching conversation is to ask the client to come up with a metaphor that captures the essence of their situation or their views. I may simply ask the client if there is a metaphor that summarises their position. Or I might ask a question such as, *'If your organisation was a high street store, which would it be and why?'*

There are also times when a metaphor or image occurs to me as I listen to a client. I then have a choice whether or not to share this. I wouldn't do this in the early stages of a coaching relationship, but if the relationship is well-established, then I might share my thoughts by saying something along the lines of, *'As you were speaking, an image came into my mind. Would you like me to share it?'* Note that a Clean Language practitioner would never do this as it's not the client's own metaphor.

Some clients enjoy playing with metaphors and find it useful, while others don't take to the idea. I remember introducing the idea of different metaphors of a leader on a leadership programme I was running at the University of Warwick. Two people from the Linguistics department loved it, while there were several engineers who wondered why on earth anyone would want to explore metaphors. (I am at risk of stereotyping in that last sentence!)

I sometimes ask participants on a coaching programme what metaphors they have for the role of a coach. A common answer is *sounding board* or *mirror*. Another theme is *guide*. You might contrast *tour guide* with *mountain guide* or with *travelling companion* – these suggest somewhat different ideas. Other metaphors include *lighthouse* or *binoculars*.

In his book *Effective Supervision for the Helping Professions*, Michael Carroll (2014) shares a number of replies to the prompt *'For me, supervision is ...'*. These include:

- a torch – which illuminates my work;
- a container – where I feel safe and held;
- a playpen – where we play with ideas, feelings, intuitions, hunches, theories.

You might take a few minutes to think what metaphors capture how you see your role as a coach, and perhaps also your metaphors for the coaching process or for supervision.

**VIDEO**

In this four-minute video Judy Rees explains more about the use of Clean Language to help a client explore their metaphors. Notice how many vivid metaphors she herself uses in the opening 20 seconds: www.youtube.com/watch?v=xJ-32O4_p14

# References

Carroll, M (2014) *Effective Supervision for the Helping Professions.* London: Sage.

Kline, N (1999) *Time to Think: Listening to Ignite the Human Mind.* London: Ward Lock.

Lakoff, G and Johnson, M (1980) *Metaphors We Live By.* Chicago: University of Chicago Press.

Lawley, J and Tompkins, P (2000) *Metaphors in Mind: Transformation through Symbolic Modelling.* London: The Developing Company Press.

Morgan, G (1996) *Images of Organization.* Thousand Oaks, CA: Sage.

Sullivan, W and Rees, J (2008) *Clean Language: Revealing Metaphors and Opening Minds.* Carmarthen: Crown House Publishing.

# Chapter 30: W

## WHY?

In Chapter 17, 'Questioning', we looked at one of the key conversational skills in coaching – asking questions to help the client understand. We noted that short, open questions are especially useful in coaching. One type of open question that can be problematic are those beginning with *Why*. In this chapter we explore this, and also look at the potential value in asking *Why?* questions.

A *Why?* question can put the client on the defensive, feeling that they have to justify themself or that they are being judged. In her book *Coaching Skills: A Handbook*, Jenny Rogers notes a number of problems:

> *The question 'why …?' invites analysis and intellectualizing.*
>
> *The 'why …?' question is also unhelpful because it often focuses on the client's motivation. Nine times out of ten when you ask this question you will get the response 'I don't know' or 'It's just how I am'.*
>
> *Similarly, 'why …?' can seem like an interrogation or an accusation. For many people it reminds us of the kinds of questions that we were asked as children by our irritated parents.*
>
> (Rogers, 2008)

The tone of voice can be very important here. You can ask a question like '*Why did you do that?*' in very different ways, some of which will come across as highly judgemental. If I want to ask a *Why?*-type question, I like to *soften* my language. For example, I might say: *'I'm wondering what led you to do that'* or *'What do you hope this will achieve?'* Note too that these two questions have a different emphasis, inviting the client to focus on distinct aspects. The first question is backward-looking and the second is forward-looking.

Another question that is likely to be problematic is *Why not?* Again, depending on the tone of voice and perhaps also on the nature of the relationship between coach and client, this type of question might be an open invitation to explore deeply, or it might be a leading question which actually is a suggestion dressed up as a question. Imagine different ways in which these questions might be heard by a client.

- Why not tell your manager what you really think?
- Why not quit your job?

Let's turn now to look at some ways in which a *Why?* question might be viewed as helpful. In a chapter on transpersonal coaching in the book *Excellence in Coaching*, Hetty Einzig and John Whitmore (2006) acknowledge concerns about *Why?* questions but argue strongly that they are important. *Transpersonal* means beyond the personal. Transpersonal coaching takes a wider, systemic view, and also embraces the spiritual dimension of a client's life. They write:

> *Why?* is a question trainee coaches are taught to avoid as it risks evoking defensiveness or explanations in the client. Transpersonal coaching is about developing a purpose-led approach to work so it does not shy away from the core question of *'What for?'* To explore why we do what we do, what our work serves and what values underpin our work helps the client understand what work means for them and what their unique contribution can be.
>
> (Einzig and Whitmore, 2006)

This quote is an interesting counter to the more widely accepted view in coaching that *Why?* questions are best avoided because they can be overly challenging and provoke defensiveness.

*Systemic coaching* is an approach that encourages the client to consider the system in which they operate and the connections between the parts of the system. In his book *Systemic Coaching and Constellations*, John Whittington defines systemic coaching as an approach that:

> coaches the individual client or team with the system in mind – exploring the part in the whole, and the whole in the part – so as to unlock the potential and performance of both.

> (Whittington, 2020)

One idea which can be useful in supporting systemic thinking is the *5 Whys technique*. Developed originally by a Japanese industrialist, Sakichi Toyoda, it has been widely used in the Toyota organisation. It's also used in approaches such as Lean Manufacturing and the Six Sigma quality improvement methodology. The approach is simple. Having identified and defined a problem, you simply ask a *Why?* question five times, aiming to identify the root cause of the problem. This is often done best as a group. It enables actions to be agreed that will address root causes rather than symptoms.

Here is an illustration from Octavio White (2018).

*Problem statement – The client refused to pay the progress payment.*

1. *Why did the client refuse to pay the progress payment? Because we completed the activity late.*

2. *Why did we complete the activity late? Because the activity took longer than estimated.*

3. *Why did the activity take longer than estimated? Because we couldn't procure enough material for the activity.*

4. *Why didn't we bring enough material? Because we didn't purchase on time.*

5. *Why didn't we purchase the materials on time? Because we didn't analyze the work schedule.*

*The root cause of the problem is that we didn't analyze the work schedule.*

*Corrective action is to create good communication channels within the project team and assemble progress meetings regularly to avoid a lack of communication and coordination.*

In her book *The Coach's Coach*, Alison Hardingham discusses a number of tools for encouraging systems thinking, including the 5 Whys. She writes:

*I don't recommend the formal 'five why's' technique for the coaching context: it is too cumbersome. But if a coach asks 'why' repeatedly it can lead to a deeper and truer understanding of a problem, and to a better basis for solving that problem.*

(Hardingham, 2004)

**REFLECTIVE TASK**

Take a little time to answer these two questions:

- What is your reaction to this chapter?
- Why is that?

## References

Einzig, H and Whitmore, J (2006) Transpersonal Coaching. In Passmore, J (ed) *Excellence in Coaching*. London: Kogan Page.

Hardingham, A (2004) *The Coach's Coach: Personal Development for Personal Developers*. London: Chartered Institute of Personnel and Development.

Rogers, J (2008) *Coaching Skills: A Handbook*. Maidenhead: McGraw Hill.

White, O (2018) 5 Whys Technique. Project Cubicle. [online] Available at: www.projectcubicle.com/5-whys-technique-5-why-analysis-examples/ (accessed 26 September 2022).

Whittington, J (2020) *Systemic Coaching and Constellations*. London: Kogan Page.

# Chapter 31: V

## VALUES IN ACTION INVENTORY OF STRENGTHS AND OTHER POSITIVE PSYCHOLOGY TOOLS

In this chapter we discuss a number of instruments and interventions from the field of Positive Psychology which you might wish to use with your coaching clients.

In the first part of his distinguished career, Martin Seligman introduced and developed the notion of *learned helplessness* – how individuals who feel they have no control over the situations they face learn to be helpless. This may result in depression or other mental illnesses.

In his Presidential Address to the American Psychological Association in 1998, Seligman set out an alternative to the established focus in psychology on mental illness and unhelpful behaviour. This initiated the development of Positive Psychology. Positive Psychology focuses on what makes life worth living, on well-being, on fulfilment and on happiness.

In their book *Character Strengths and Virtues: A Handbook and Classification*, Christopher Peterson and Martin Seligman say:

*We write from the perspective of positive psychology, which means that we are as focused on strength as on weakness, as interested in building the best things in life as in repairing the worst, and as concerned with fulfilling the lives of normal people as with healing the wounds of the distressed ... we believe that character strengths are the bedrock of the human condition and that strength-congruent activity represents an important route to the psychological good life.*

(Peterson and Seligman, 2004)

In their chapter in the book *Mastery in Coaching*, Lindsay Oades and Jonathan Passmore offer this definition of Positive Psychology coaching:

*coaching approaches that seek to improve short-term wellbeing ... and sustainable wellbeing ... using evidence-based approaches from positive psychology and the science of wellbeing and enable the person to do this in an ongoing manner after coaching has completed.*

(Oades and Passmore, 2014)

Let's look now at two self-assessment instruments which seek to help an individual to identify their strengths. The Values in Action Inventory of Strengths (VIA-IS) was developed by Peterson and Seligman in 2004. The VIA-IS was part of this move within psychology to explore what is 'right' in people rather than what is 'wrong' with them, to look at strengths rather than weaknesses. Peterson and Seligman hoped that the VIA-IS would be a manual for Positive Psychology that was equivalent to the American Psychiatric Association's Diagnostic and Statistical Manual (DSM), which contains descriptions, symptoms and other criteria necessary for diagnosing mental health disorders. They hoped that it would be the foundation for a science of human strengths.

The VIA-IS is a free self-assessment tool that has been completed by more than 15 million people. It seeks to identify an individual's profile of character strengths. You can complete your own assessment by following this link: www.viacharacter.org. The website states that:

*Character strengths are positive traits – capacities humans have for thinking, feeling, and behaving in ways that benefit*

*oneself and others. Specifically, they are the psychological*
*ingredients for displaying virtues or human goodness.*

(VIA Institute on Character, nd)

As shown in Table 31.1, the VIA-IS consists of 24 character
strengths, arranged within six virtues. Each of us possesses all
of the strengths, in different degrees, which creates a unique
character strengths profile.

**Table 31.1 The Values in Action Inventory of Strengths**

| Virtue | Strength |
|---|---|
| Wisdom | Creativity<br>Curiosity<br>Judgement<br>Love of learning<br>Perspective |
| Courage | Bravery<br>Perseverance<br>Honesty<br>Zest |
| Humanity | Love<br>Kindness<br>Social intelligence |
| Justice | Teamwork<br>Fairness<br>Leadership |
| Temperance | Forgiveness<br>Humility<br>Prudence<br>Self-regulation |
| Transcendence | Appreciation of beauty and excellence<br>Gratitude<br>Hope<br>Humour<br>Spirituality |

Another free self-assessment tool is the Strengths Profile, which you can complete via this link: www.strengthsprofile.com. This lists 60 different strengths. One feature of this instrument is that, based on how you answer the questions, your profile separates out your:

- *realised strengths*: these are strengths that you use and enjoy using – use these wisely;
- *unrealised strengths*: these are strengths you don't use as often – use these more;
- *learned behaviour*: these are things you do well but may not enjoy doing – use these when needed;
- *weaknesses*: these are things you find hard and don't enjoy – use these less.

Both the Values in Action Inventory and the Strengths Profile can be used within coaching to help a client to perform more effectively, enhance their relationships or find a more satisfying career by focusing on their strengths and what they enjoy doing. It is often more useful to build upon and enhance strengths than to address or correct weaknesses. This may be particularly relevant in helping someone explore their future career direction – they're likely to be more successful and happier following a path that plays to their strengths. Both of the tools can also be used to work with the members of a team, helping them to appreciate each other's strengths and how to capitalise on these to make the team more effective.

For four years I was the external examiner for the MSc in Applied Positive Psychology and Coaching Psychology at the University of East London. The MSc integrates Positive Psychology and coaching psychology to create an innovative degree programme for participants who wish to use coaching to promote well-being. In moderating assignments submitted for assessment by the students, I read about a variety of Positive Psychological Interventions (PPIs) that coaches can use with clients to enhance their well-being and effectiveness. There is a detailed description and discussion of PPIs on the PositivePsychology.com website, which states that

> *Positive psychology interventions, or PPIs, are a set of scientific tools and strategies that focus on increasing happiness, wellbeing, and positive cognitions and emotions.*
> (Chowdhury, 2022)

In their chapter in *The Complete Handbook of Coaching*, Carol Kauffman, Ilona Boniwell and Jordan Silberman describe a number of these PPIs. Here are some examples to give a flavour.

- ***Three good things***: *Every night, just before going to sleep, write down three things that went well during the day.*

- ***Gratitude visit:*** *Draft a letter to someone to whom you feel gratitude for something they did in the past. Arrange to meet them, and then read the letter aloud to them.*

- ***Savouring:*** *Noticing and savouring life's pleasures, both subtle and spectacular, can powerfully enhance well-being. Focus intentionally on positive experiences in your daily life.*

- ***Best possible future self:*** *Imagine that everything has gone the way you wanted, and all your goals have been realised. Vividly imagine this future.*

- ***Using your strengths in a new way:*** *Choose a top strength, and apply it in a new way, every day, for one week.*
  (Kauffman et al, 2010)

Inviting a coaching client to do exercises such as these, and reviewing their experience at your next coaching session, can help them to feel more positive in their daily life and to cope better with negative events or moods that they may experience.

You can also read more about PPIs in a chapter entitled 'Positive Psychological Interventions: An Overview' by Acacia Parks and Liudmila Titova (2016).

**VIDEO**

In this 24-minute TED talk Martin Seligman reflects on the success of the traditional disease-based approach to psychology and psychiatry, and then goes on to set out fundamental ideas in the alternative approach of Positive Psychology. The first few minutes are a very amusing introduction to set up the talk: www.youtube.com/watch?v= 9FBxfd7DL3E

## References

Chowdhury, M (2022) 19 Best Positive Psychology Interventions and How to Apply Them. [online] Available at: https://positive psychology.com/positive-psychology-interventions/ (accessed 26 September 2022).

Kauffman, C, Boniwell, I and Silberman, J (2010) The Positive Psychology Approach to Coaching. In Cox, E, Bachkirova, T and Clutterbuck, D (eds) *The Complete Handbook of Coaching* (pp 158–71). London: Sage.

Oades, L and Passmore, J (2014) Positive Psychology Coaching. In Passmore, J (ed) *Mastery in Coaching* (pp 15–40). London: Kogan Page.

Parks, A and Titova, L (2016) Positive Psychological Interventions: An Overview. In Wood, A and Johnson, J (eds) *The Wiley Handbook of Positive Clinical Psychology* (pp 307–20). Chichester: Wiley.

Peterson, C and Seligman, M (2004) *Character Strengths and Virtues: A Handbook and Classification*. Oxford: Oxford University Press.

VIA Institute on Character (nd) Bring Your Strengths to Life and Live More Fully. [online] Available at: www.viacharacter.org (accessed 26 September 2022).

# Chapter 32: U

## USE OF SELF

In *The Four Aspects to a Coaching Session*, Peter Bluckert writes:

> *I regard the use of self as the highest order coaching skill. It can be the key difference between good and great coaching...*
>
> *In my view techniques have their place but the most important tool of all is yourself. Your self. In the search for toolkits many aspiring and practicing coaches miss this fundamental point.*
>
> (Bluckert, 2004)

In this chapter we look at a number of ways in which you might use your self in your coaching conversations, moving into more depth as we go.

A very simple consideration is whether or not you'll disclose any personal information about yourself to your client. Some counsellors, for example, take care not to display any family photographs in their office as this might suggest some kind of judgement about the value of family life. In my own practice, I'm happy to share some details of myself and my interests when I begin working with a new client. Taking a few minutes to introduce ourselves to one another sometimes establishes some form of mutual interest or connection.

A key issue for you to consider, which we've discussed in a number of chapters, is how directive or non-directive you wish to be in your practice. Offering advice, guidance or suggestions to a client must, to a greater or lesser extent, come from your view of the world. In many mentoring relationships, this might be exactly what the mentee is looking for. In Rogerian counselling, on the other hand, this is regarded as utterly inappropriate. I describe my own practice as primarily non-directive. I will very occasionally offer a suggestion – hopefully with clarity on why I'm choosing to do this.

You also have a choice about whether or not to share your own experiences with a client. You may have been in a similar situation in the past. For example, perhaps the client has just been made redundant and you've been in that position yourself. You may have some useful ideas to share. On the other hand, you are not your client, and there will be important differences in the client's situation – and personality – from yours.

Another issue is whether and how you give feedback to a client. You inevitably notice things in the client that they may or may not be aware of – body language, tone of voice, their precise words, patterns of thinking or habits of behaving, etc. You continually have a choice as to what, if anything, to highlight to the client. In Chapter 6, 'Feedback', we distinguished between *giving* and *generating* feedback. I prefer to ask the client what they think is working well or less well, for example, so that they generate their own feedback. But I am prepared to give – judiciously, I hope – feedback when appropriate. Again, you have a choice about what you will do in your own practice.

In *Use of Self in Executive Coaching*, Michael Frisch offers this definition, which is about using oneself at a much deeper level than we've considered so far:

> *A coach's thought or feeling reaction to a client that the coach is both aware of and will use, either directly or indirectly, in the service of the coaching.*
>
> (Frisch, 2008, p 13)

When you notice some thoughts or feelings that have arisen for you yourself (rather than the client) in a coaching conversation, you again have a choice what to do. You might do nothing, or you might mentally make a note for the time being, or you might share your thought or feeling with the client. In *The Use of Self and Self Disclosure in Coaching*, Marjorie Shackleton and Marion Gillie offer these guidelines.

- The key question that guides your decision is always *'how will your disclosure serve the client?'* (For example, will it heighten the client's awareness?)
- If you are unsure then wait, and by delaying you may get further clarity about your internal data, which might well be of use to the client at a later point in the session.
- If a feeling, image, etc, *has* persisted with this client during the session or over the time you have known him or her, it is important you choose to disclose when it emerges once more in the current session.

If you decide to share what's coming up for you, it's vital to choose your words carefully. It's important to be non-judgemental, and also not to interpret what your reaction might signify.

Having a high degree of self-awareness is essential if you wish to use what's arising for you in the service of a client. You need to be able to distinguish what's your *stuff*, as it were, and what might be the client's. As an illustration, let's say you notice a sense of frustration in yourself while the client is speaking. This might be because you yourself would feel frustrated if you were in the client's situation. Or it might be because the client is sharing lots of irrelevant detail. Or it might be that you are picking up that the client is feeling frustrated – and perhaps does not realise this – in their own situation. If you decide to respond, you might say something along the lines of: *'As you were speaking, I had a feeling of frustration. I wonder what that might signify?'*

This self-awareness – together with awareness of what's emerging for the client and the working relationship as the conversation unfolds – links with the idea of *presence*. The website of the International Coach Federation (ICF) includes a set of core competences for a coach. One of these is *Maintains Presence*, which they define as '*Is fully conscious and present with the client, employing a style that is open, flexible, grounded and confident.*' They list these six aspects.

1. *Remains focused, observant, empathetic and responsive to the client.*

2. *Demonstrates curiosity during the coaching process.*

3. *Manages one's emotions to stay present with the client.*

4. *Demonstrates confidence in working with strong client emotions during the coaching process.*

5. *Is comfortable working in a space of not knowing.*

6. *Creates or allows space for silence, pause or reflection.*

(ICF, 2019)

In a chapter on the Gestalt supervision model, Marion Gillie writes these words (which apply to a coach as well as a supervisor):

*Presence is much more than how 'professional' you are as a supervisor. It includes how 'grounded' you are in yourself and your work, how able you are to 'contact' the client, even when they are difficult to reach. It is the ability to be in the here and now, ie to tune into what is going on within yourself (your reactions to your supervisees, what they evoke in you, what images come to mind, what sensations are stimulated) as you are impacted by them, and to disclose some of this in order to 'make contact'.*

(Gillie, 2011)

In his book *The Coaching Relationship in Practice*, Geoff Pelham writes:

> *As I enter more deeply into the relationship the use of self tends to shift from 'technique' to a genuine sharing of what is going on for me.*
>
> (Pelham, 2016)

---

**REFLECTIVE TASK**

- Reflecting upon your own practice with your clients, in what ways do you use your self in your coaching?
- How might you use your self differently?

---

## References

Bluckert, P (2004) *The Four Dimensions to a Coaching Session*. Littleport: Fenman.

Frisch, M (2008) *Use of Self in Executive Coaching*. New York: i-Coach Coaching Monograph Series. [online] Available at: https://icoachnewyork.com/wp-content/uploads/2015/09/Monograph.pdf (accessed 24 August 2022).

Gillie, M (2011) The Gestalt Supervision Model. In Passmore, J (ed) *Supervision in Coaching* (pp 45–63). London: Kogan Page.

ICF (2019) Updated ICF Core Competencies. [online] Available at: https://coachingfederation.org/app/uploads/2021/03/ICF-Core-Competencies-updated.pdf (accessed 26 September 2022).

Pelham, G (2016) *The Coaching Relationship in Practice*. London: Sage.

Shackleton, M and Gillie, M (2010) *The Use of Self and Self Disclosure in Coaching*. AoEC Conference 2010.

# Chapter 33: T

## TIME MANAGEMENT

---

A topic that frequently arises in coaching conversations is time management. Many clients struggle to manage their time well or to achieve the work–life balance that they want. In this chapter we look at a number of ideas or frameworks that you might share with a coaching client who wants to manage their time more effectively.

An idea that I believe is fundamental for effective time management is to be clear about your priorities – and then to spend your time in ways that reflect these. The 'urgent–important matrix' shown in Figure 33.1 is a useful framework to help a client to think through the various activities that take up their time, placing them on the grid.

Figure 33.1  The urgent–important matrix

|  | NOT IMPORTANT | IMPORTANT |
|---|---|---|
| URGENT |  |  |
| NOT URGENT |  |  |

Most of us are good at doing the things that are important and urgent. When a crisis hits, we respond. And many of us spend time on things that feel urgent but aren't that important. Just because a meeting is in your calendar doesn't make it important, but we often think that we have to attend. What distinguishes people who are very good at managing their time is that they invest time in doing the things that are important but not yet urgent. Activities like planning, delegating, building relationships and recharging your batteries can often be put off – they're not urgent today. But, if you keep putting them off, they might never get done – or only get done once they become urgent.

When coaching someone who has problems with time management, I may ask them to list the various tasks that they need to do, and then to place them on the grid. I often find that they regard almost everything as important. But some things must be more important than others – they can't all be equally important!

The ability to say *no* is a valuable skill in time management, and also in behaving assertively. I like a quote from the American billionaire and philanthropist Warren Buffet, who said that, '*The difference between successful people and very successful people is that very successful people say "no" to almost everything.*' I've recently said *no* to two invitations from colleagues (whom I work well with) to sit on interview panels. While I want to support my colleagues, I'm balancing helping them, on the one hand, with spending time on my own priorities.

There are also meetings that I'm invited to but which I judge to be relatively unimportant. I mean unimportant in terms of my priorities – the meetings might be important in the priorities of others. At the end of the day, you are the judge of what your priorities are. You have to live with the consequences of, for example, saying *no* to a meeting that your boss or a client considers important. And, if you say *no* to everything you're asked to do, you might well find yourself out of work. I have a '*rule of three*' for some regular meetings. I reckon it's politically unwise never to attend, but my attendance is rarely of value. So, I turn up for around one in three of such meetings.

Once you've decided what's more important or less important, it can be useful to set aside explicitly time to work on your priority areas. For example, perhaps you want to create a strategy document to revise the service that your department offers. This is important, but probably not urgent – you don't need to start on it this week. It can be useful to block out time in your calendar to work on the strategy – for instance, you might set aside Thursdays for the next ten weeks. And then, unless some genuine crisis emerges, make sure that you do spend your Thursdays on the strategy, rather than being drawn into less important meetings or maybe simply going through your emails. Focusing on what's really important, and setting aside time for this, can be summed up in the phrase '*Schedule your priorities, don't prioritise your schedule.*'

Another useful skill in managing your time is the ability to delegate, to ask someone else to carry out a task. Investing time in delegating can free you up to concentrate on more important activities. I find this checklist useful when asking someone to do something.

- Are they *clear* about what I'm asking them to do?
- Are they *capable* – perhaps with some training or support – of doing it?
- Are they *confident* about taking it on?
- Are they *committed* to doing the task?

You need to be able to tick all four in order to delegate. And, depending on which item is absent, you need to intervene differently. If someone is unclear, you may explain things again – but this is irrelevant if what's missing is commitment.

One area that often consumes a lot of time is handling emails. I find an idea that I call *Clear Your Inbox* useful. There are only four things you can do with an email.

1. You can *delete* it – it's not relevant.
2. You can *reply* quickly to it – and move it out of your inbox.
3. You can *forward* it to someone else, either to handle it or for information – again it's out of your inbox.
4. You may have to *do some work to respond* to the email. A two-line email might create six months of work! Make a note in whatever form of *To do* list you have, and file the email in an appropriate folder so that you can access it later. Again, the email is out of your inbox.

A final time management idea that I sometimes share with coaching clients is called *Eat that Frog*, from the title of a book by Brian Tracy (2001). If you have a difficult or unpleasant task, it's easy to postpone it, to procrastinate. Tracy calls such tasks *Frogs*, and recommends that you tackle these first thing in the morning. This hopefully gets them out of the way, freeing you up to work on other, perhaps more interesting, things for the rest of the day. As an illustration, if you have to phone the dentist to make an appointment, do it early in the day.

In sharing these ideas in coaching, I find that clients often see the value in them. It is then over to them to act in response. Having good intentions isn't enough – they need to carry these out. Remember that it's Awareness *plus* Responsibility that produces Performance.

**VIDEO**

Stephen Covey's book *The 7 Habits of Highly Effective People* (1989) is a classic best-seller that offers great ideas and examples on how to manage your time effectively to pursue the goals that are important and meaningful to you. This seven-minute animated video is a succinct summary of the seven habits: www.youtube.com/watch?v=ktlT xC4QG8g

## References

Covey, S (1989) *The 7 Habits of Highly Effective People*. London: Simon & Schuster.

Tracy, B (2001) *Eat that Frog*. San Francisco, CA: Berrett-Koehler.

# Chapter 34: S

## SOLUTION-FOCUSED COACHING

In a sense, all coaching is solution focused. Coaching aims to help a client to clarify and achieve their goals. The GROW model, for example, is a framework to do just this. Solution-focused coaching is an approach with a number of distinctive features, which we explore in this chapter.

A solution-focused approach to coaching evolved from a solution-focused approach to therapy. Working with families at the Brief Therapy Centre in Milwaukee, Steve de Shazer and Insoo Kim Berg observed that families who argued about problems and about who was to blame made little progress. Inviting them to focus on what they wanted and on times when things were going well led to greater and faster progress (de Shazer et al, 2021).

In their chapter in the *Handbook of Coaching Psychology*, Bill O'Connell and Stephen Palmer write:

> *Solution-focused coaching (SFC) is an outcome-oriented, competence-based approach. It helps clients to achieve their preferred outcomes by evoking and co-constructing solutions to their problems. SFC fits perfectly with the future-focused, goal-directed sprit of coaching. Rather than problem-solve, the solution-focused coach gives centre stage to the skills, strengths, knowledge and experience of the client.*
>
> (O'Connell and Palmer, 2007)

Here are some of the key characteristics of solution-focused coaching.

- As in many other approaches to coaching, a solution-focused coach aims to create a respectful and collaborative relationship with the client.
- The coach doesn't view the client as dysfunctional or ill, and doesn't attempt to diagnose what's wrong with them.
- While the coach may listen as the client talks about problems or things that happened in the past, they will seek to move the client on to explore constructive ways forward.
- The coach views the client as resourceful, capable of setting personal goals and of identifying ways of achieving these. The client is the expert about their own life. They understand their own hopes and fears, and know what has worked for them in the past and what they are prepared to do in the future.
- The coach will work with the expectation that positive change will occur, and help the client to define clear, specific goals. They also expect the client to work on their goals outside of the coaching session.

Let's look at a number of tools used in solution-focused coaching. These can also be used in other approaches to coaching.

Helping the client to *reframe* how they view things is a central idea in solution-focused coaching. A classic if somewhat clichéd illustration of reframing is seeing the glass as half-full rather than half-empty. It may be that the coach asks the client to reframe things by, for example, simply asking how they could view things differently or what they see as the positive aspects of a situation. As an illustration, if the client says, *'I'm not getting on with my boss anymore'*, the coach might respond with, *'Tell me what you were doing when you were getting on with your boss.'*

Alternatively, the coach could offer a reframe to the client. For example, speaking to a client who has recently lost their job, the coach might ask a question such as, *'What opportunities might this open up for you?'*

In solution-focused coaching, reframing is captured in the maxim *'Change the viewing to change the doing.'* In their chapter in

*Excellence in Coaching,* Anthony Grant, Sean O'Connor and Ingrid Studholme write:

> *Changing the viewing is about acknowledging the progress made so far, identifying exceptions to the problem, detailing the preferred outcome, amplifying existing resources and building coachee self-efficacy. Essentially, changing the viewing is about shifting perspectives that the coachee may have in relation to their problem, issue, situation and goal that may be assumptive or unhelpful, to more effective approaches that support them towards their vision or desired future.*
>
> (Grant et al, 2021)

In *The Coach's Coach*, Alison Hardingham (2004) makes this important point: *'Reframes that don't speak to people's underlying values, beliefs and motives won't work.'*

A solution-focused coach will encourage the client to carry out tasks or assignments between sessions, which they'll review in the next session. These can assist the client to do the work they need to do in order to make the changes they seek. O'Connell and Palmer (2007) note some useful principles for selecting some of these tasks.

- If it works keep doing it.
- If it doesn't work stop doing it.
- Small steps can lead to big changes.
- Do something different.

Asking a *scaling question* is often employed in solution-focused coaching. As an illustration, here is a scaling question together with a follow-up question inviting the client to think about achievable next steps.

> Coach: *On a scale of one to ten, how confident are you feeling about next week's presentation?*

Client: *About a five.*

Coach: *What would it take for you to be at a six?*

Another question asked by solution-focused coaches is known as the *miracle question*. This encourages the client to consider what things would be like if a miracle happened and their problems disappeared. Note that some clients might not like the notion of a miracle, perhaps because it may have religious connotations for them. Putting it another way, the question is an invitation to the client to imagine that they've successfully achieved their goal and to describe what success looks like. So, you might ask, '*Imagine that everything has worked out exactly as you want. What will you be seeing, doing and feeling?*' Another way in which I pose what is effectively the miracle question is to invite the client to draw a rich picture of what life will be like if everything works out as they would wish it to.

It's important to choose a suitable point in the conversation to ask the miracle question. Asking it while the client is still describing what's wrong may confuse or irritate them – it's better to wait until the client has started to focus on solutions and actions.

An integrative coach is prepared to draw on ideas from a variety of approaches. These ideas in solution-focused coaching sit comfortably with other approaches and with an integrative approach. Coming from a primarily non-directive approach to coaching, I myself feel comfortable using some of these ideas in my own practice.

Grant, O'Connor and Studholme end their chapter with these words:

> *Its primary focus on outcomes over analysis may seem simplistic to some, but the solution-focused approach takes pride in keeping it simple. Staying focused on solutions is the essence of great coaching. Simple may not always mean easy!*
> (Grant et al, 2021)

**VIDEO AND READING**

The link below contains a short introduction to a solution-focused approach to therapy, a worksheet outlining 20 solution-focused techniques and a short animated video discussing the value of an emphasis on solutions rather than problems. The introduction states:

> *solution focused work can be seen as a way of working that focuses exclusively or predominantly on two things:*
>
> 1. *Supporting people to explore their preferred futures.*
> 2. *Exploring when, where, with whom and how pieces of that preferred future are already happening.*

www.familyseparationhub.net/information-for-practitioners/learning-zone-1/solution-focussed-practice/

This website contains a link to a downloadable pdf of the worksheet.

# References

de Shazer, S, Dolan, Y, Korman, H, Trepper, T, McCollum, E and Berg, I K (2021) *More Than Miracles: The State of the Art of Solution-Focused Brief Therapy*. New York: Routledge.

Grant, A, O'Connor, S and Studholme, I (2021) Solution-focused Coaching. In Passmore, J (ed) *Excellence in Coaching* (4th edition, pp 121–42). London: Kogan Page.

Hardingham, A (2004) *The Coach's Coach: Personal Development for Personal Developers*. London: Chartered Institute of Personnel and Development.

O'Connell, B and Palmer, S (2007) Solution-focused Coaching. In Palmer, S and Whybrow, A (eds) *Handbook of Coaching Psychology* (pp 278–92). London: Routledge.

# Chapter 35: R

## ROLL WITH RESISTANCE – IDEAS FROM MOTIVATIONAL INTERVIEWING

As you progress along your journey as a coach, you'll encounter new ideas and may wish to assimilate some of these into your own practice. I first heard about Motivational Interviewing (MI) by chance in a conversation during a coffee break on a supervision workshop. It was a good example of finding an approach that was new to me and which seemed to fit well into my own style of primarily non-directive coaching. I learnt more about it by reading the classic book on the subject, *Motivational Interviewing: Preparing People for Change* by William Miller and Stephen Rollnick.

Miller and Rollnick (2002) define MI as *'a client-centered, directive method for enhancing intrinsic motivation to change by exploring and resolving ambivalence'*. Each of these terms is carefully chosen, and it's worth unpicking them.

- *MI is client-centred.* The coach respects the client as an autonomous person, and responsibility for change rests with the client.
- *MI is directive.* Miller developed the approach from his therapeutic work with problem drinkers. There is a direction in which the client needs to go – to drink less or no alcohol – and the therapist or coach is supporting the client to go in that direction. Similarly, with clients who have drug problems or are obese or are sex offenders, there is a preferred direction.
- *MI enhances intrinsic motivation to change.* The term *Motivational Interviewing* reflects the belief that the

motivation has to come from the client. If the coach tries to push the client, that is unlikely to be effective and indeed may well provoke resistance.

- *MI explores and resolves ambivalence.* Helping the client to work through their ambivalence – *I want to change, but I don't want to change* – is the key challenge. If the client is clear that they want to change, then an approach such as solution-focused or cognitive behavioural coaching may well be more suitable than MI.

There is a lovely line in the book about ambivalence: *'Ambivalence is a reasonable place to visit, but you wouldn't want to live there'* (Miller and Rollnick, 2002).

MI shares some fundamental principles with a Rogerian person-centred approach. In both approaches, it is vital to demonstrate to the client empathic understanding and non-judgemental acceptance. Listening respectfully to the client, without judging, criticising or blaming them, enables them to explore their ambivalence. Paradoxically, accepting people as they are seems to free them to change.

How the coach responds to resistance is the hallmark of Motivational Interviewing. When the client is resisting change and presenting arguments against change, it is important that the coach does not oppose this, which is likely to be counterproductive. Rather, the coach works with the client's resistance, acknowledging that ambivalence is natural. The coach needs to *roll with the resistance*.

Miller and Rollnick (2002) write that:

*Resistance lies at the very heart of human change. It arises from the motives and struggles of the actors. It foreshadows certain ends to which the play may or may not lead. The true art of a counselor is tested in the recognition and handling of resistance. It is on this stage that the drama of change unfolds.*

When the client is resistant, this is a signal for the coach, not the client, to do something different.

MI differs from a Rogerian person-centred approach by deliberately aiming to help the client to resolve their ambivalence and move towards positive behavioural change. An MI coach will intentionally invite the client to amplify any discrepancy between their current state and where they want to be.

In order to change, the client needs to believe in the possibility for change. The coach supports and encourages the client's belief in their ability to carry out their plans successfully, and seeks to enhance the client's confidence that they can make the changes they desire. Ultimately, of course, it is up to the client to change – the coach can only help them to do so.

In MI it is the client not the coach who must present the arguments for change. The coach's skill in *eliciting change talk* is the key strategy for developing discrepancy, resolving ambivalence and encouraging change. When the coach hears the client begin to talk of change, they invite the client to explore this further. Eliciting change talk is intentionally directive, seeking to tip the balance in the direction of the change desired by the client. Note that this is not about manipulating the client nor about the coach setting the direction for change.

MI can be thought of as involving two phases with different but overlapping goals. In phase one, the coach helps the client to explore and resolve their ambivalence, building their motivation for change. When the client seems *'willing and able to change and is on the brink of readiness'* (Miller and Rollnick, 2002), the coach moves the conversation on to help the client to set goals, consider options, create a plan and commit to change.

You might view this as walking up a mountain and then going down the other slope. With a highly ambivalent client who isn't ready to change, the work of phase one – going up the mountain – may be difficult and take a lot of time. With some clients, progress down the other side might be straightforward – it may be obvious to a client who has resolved their ambivalence what they are going to do. Alternatively, as the client explores how to create their change plan, ambivalence may return – and the coach needs to help the client explore this.

So far, we have discussed MI in a context where there is a preferred direction for the client to go. However, it can also be used in more neutral contexts when there isn't an obviously more desirable state. For example, a client might be feeling stuck on whether or not to accept a job offer or stay in their current role, and the coach can use the ideas above to help them to explore both options. In Chapter 16, 'Playing back', we noted the useful MI technique of double-sided reflection when the coach simply plays back accurately and without judgement both halves of a client's dilemma. So, in this example, the coach might say something along these lines:

*On the one hand, the new job means more money and a fresh challenge. On the other hand, you are really enjoying your current work, feeling that it's making a real contribution.*

### VIDEO

In this seven-minute video Stephen Rollnick demonstrates very effectively how to convey empathic understanding and acceptance to a patient who is angry. He is seeking to *engage* the patient, hoping that he will recognise and, in time, address the issue that he is severely overweight. The process of *engaging* is vital because good engagement between doctor and patient – or coach and client – is essential in order to have a purposeful conversation about change.

In terms of the metaphor of going up and down the mountain, the conversation in the video is mainly in the phase of going up the mountain: www.youtube.com/watch?v=bTRRNWrwRCo

The link also includes a further link to a free *British Medical Journal* learning course, 'Motivational interviewing in brief consultations', that you can register for.

## Reference

Miller, W and Rollnick, S (2002) *Motivational Interviewing: Preparing People for Change.* New York: Guilford Press.

# Chapter 36: Q

## QUALIFICATIONS AND ACCREDITATION

Anyone starting out to learn how to coach is likely to consider which workshops or programmes to attend. And later, as they enhance their skills and confidence, they may well take part in further learning opportunities. Some may also wish to gain a formal qualification in coaching. And some may seek formal accreditation by one of the coaching bodies. In this chapter we discuss these possibilities – choosing a programme, obtaining a qualification and gaining accreditation.

There are now countless coaching programmes to choose from. Some are run by commercial organisations, while others are offered by colleges and universities. If you are thinking of signing up for one, here are some key questions to consider.

- *Practicalities.* How long is the course? How much is delivered face-to-face, and how much is online? If there is face-to-face delivery, how convenient is the venue for you? Is there any residential element?
- *Cost.* What are the fees? What other costs, such as books, travel or accommodation, will you incur? How does it rate in terms of value for money?
- *Facilitation.* Who are the people who facilitate the programme? What experience do they have of doing coaching themselves or of supervising others? Do they favour a particular approach to coaching?
- *Participants.* Who else will be taking part, and what kind of background and experience do they have? You are likely to learn

a lot from fellow participants, and you may go on to develop working partnerships or friendships with some of them.

- *Opportunity to coach.* What opportunities are included in the design of the course to enable you to gain experience of coaching? This might be coaching fellow participants, or it might involve finding and coaching practice clients, or it might be drawing on your day-to-day experiences.
- *Assessment.* Does the course involve any written assessment? Does it involve any assessment of your coaching skills? If the course leads to an award, which body gives the award?
- *Qualification.* Does successful completion of the course give you some form of qualification? And does it contribute to the requirements needed for formal accreditation by one of the coaching bodies? We return to this point below.

There are other ways in which you can build your coaching knowledge and skills. Bodies such as the Association for Coaching, the European Mentoring and Coaching Council (EMCC) and the International Coaching Federation offer a variety of opportunities, including podcasts, webinars on specific topics (which may be a single session or a series of sessions), co-coaching forums (where you can not only coach and be coached but also network with like-minded coaches) and conferences. In Chapter 19, 'Supervision', we looked at the value of having a place where you can take time out to reflect upon and develop your practice. There are also books, magazines and journals offering a variety of ideas to stimulate your thinking and your practice.

An easy step on your coaching journey is to become a member of one of the coaching bodies. I've noted the three main ones in the previous paragraph, but there are others too. Applying for membership via the relevant website is easy and not that expensive – typically there is an annual membership fee. You'll then have access to the resources on their website and to the events and opportunities they offer.

Seeking accreditation from one of the coaching bodies is a larger step, one that may require a fair amount of work as you put together your application. I myself am accredited as a senior practitioner coach and also as a supervisor by the EMCC. I'll discuss accreditation using the EMCC as an example, but similar remarks will apply to accreditation by other bodies. Their websites will give full details of how to apply, and also of the support available to help you put together your application.

The EMCC has four levels of mentor/coach accreditation – Foundation, Practitioner, Senior Practitioner and Master Practitioner. You need to submit details and evidence for the criteria below – the requirements to meet the criteria increase for the different levels of accreditation:

- *Length of experience*

- *Number of client contact hours*

- *Number of clients*

- *Feedback from clients*

- *Continuing professional development*

- *Your own supervision*

- *Reflection on your practice*

- *Membership of a professional body.*

(EMCC, nd)

You also have to provide evidence of your competence. You can do this by sharing case studies of your work with clients that demonstrate that you meet the competences set out in the EMCC's competency framework. However, you don't need to do this if you have gained a certificate from an EMCC-accredited training programme. You may want to bear this in mind when you are choosing a training programme.

While putting together your application takes some care and time, it is also an opportunity to reflect systematically upon your practice. Putting down in writing your reflections can help you to clarify your strengths and weaknesses, to make explicit some of the challenges you face, and to suggest next steps for your continuing development as a coach.

For many participants on a programme, the reason for attending is to learn and develop, and perhaps to network. Some people also wish to obtain a qualification. And some qualifications, as we've illustrated, ease the path to accreditation. You may consider that having a qualification and/or accreditation will be useful in winning business as a coach. It is an indication – although not a guarantee – of a level of quality. And some purchasers of coaching services wish to employ coaches who have a qualification or are accredited by one of the coaching bodies. In her book *Coaching Presence*, Maria Iliffe-Wood writes:

> *Some clients are not interested in qualifications, all they want to know is – can you help me? It can depend on the size of business you want to engage with. The bigger the business the more likely you are to be asked for qualifications.*
>
> *The same companies that might ask for qualifications might also require coaches they employ to be accredited by one of the professional bodies.*
>
> (Iliffe-Wood, 2014)

As we noted earlier, one of the criteria required for accreditation by EMCC is continuing professional development (CPD). Whether or not you wish to be accredited, CPD is important in keeping your practice fresh, in evolving your approach over time and ultimately in offering a great service to your clients.

REFLECTIVE **TASK**

Here are some questions inviting you to reflect upon your continuing development as a coach.

Make some notes about your current level of skill, confidence and activity as a coach, and also on where you'd like to be in, say, two or three years' time.

- In what areas do you want to develop yourself as a coach?
- For each of these areas, what might you do to develop?
- How relevant or useful will it be for you to obtain a coaching qualification over this period?
- How relevant or useful will it be for you to gain formal accreditation as a coach over this period?
- Bringing this together, what actions will you take to further your development as a coach?
- What deadlines will you set in regard to these actions?
- When and how will you review your progress?

# References

EMCC (nd) About EMCC Global Individual Accreditation (EIA). [online] Available at: www.emccglobal.org/accreditation/eia/ (accessed 26 September 2022).

Iliffe-Wood, M (2014) *Coaching Presence*. London: Kogan Page.

# Chapter 37: P

## PSYCHOMETRIC INSTRUMENTS AND 360-DEGREE FEEDBACK

In the opening chapter we discussed how you might summarise the essence of coaching in the equation:

Awareness + responsibility = performance

One thing you might do with a coaching client to raise their self-awareness is to invite them to complete a psychometric instrument or test. There are many of these to choose from – some are free and easily available on the internet, some require payment and others can only be used by someone who has been trained and accredited to use them. Tools available include personality tests, aptitude tests and questionnaires assessing strengths, values, interests, leadership and motivational needs. In the book *Psychometrics in Coaching*, edited by Jonathan Passmore (2008), you can read about important considerations in the design and use of psychometric instruments and about a range of different tools.

Many of the tools are self-report instruments where an individual assesses themself against a range of questions. This means that the results – and any written reports that are automatically generated based on these results – are purely a product of their own inputs. So, if they are answering inaccurately, or if their answers are overly influenced by recent events or maybe even how they're feeling when they input their responses, this can skew the results. Nevertheless, taking someone through their results – like holding a mirror up to them – will probably stimulate useful reflections and awareness.

In Chapter 31, we discussed the Values in Action Inventory of Strengths self-assessment tool, which reports an individual's profile of character strengths. And in Chapter 24, 'Extraverts and Introverts', we looked at the Myers-Briggs Type Indicator (MBTI), a self-assessment tool that is the most widely used personality test in the world.

The LeadershipPlus module that I run on the full-time MBA at Warwick Business School invites the students to explore personal effectiveness, teamwork and leadership. One idea that I share at the beginning of the module is the notion that *who you are is how you lead*. Self-awareness is vital in leadership. To help them develop this, we ask each student to complete the Insights Discovery Profile. This is based on three of the four dimensions of the MBTI. The Insights website summarises the profile in these words:

> *The Insights Discovery methodology uses a simple and memorable four colour model to help people understand their style, their strengths and the value they bring to the team. We call these the colour energies, and it's the unique mix of Fiery Red, Sunshine Yellow, Earth Green and Cool Blue energies, which determines how and why people behave the way they do.*

(Insights, nd)

The MBA students find the use of the four colours a very helpful way of describing both themself and their syndicate colleagues. It creates a common language to help them to get to know each other and to take due account of individual strengths and weaknesses. They can also see a group profile that summarises the overall strengths and weaknesses of their syndicate. An important point in regard to Insights is that each of us possesses all four energies, and we can modify our behaviour to draw upon our less preferred energies. However, a downside of the four-colour typology is that students often oversimplify things, caricaturing individuals as, say, just a *Red* or a *Blue*.

Some instruments are based on a combination of self-reporting and the views of other people who know the individual. A common version of this is 360-degree feedback where responses are collected from the individual, their line manager, the people who report to the person and others, such as peers or customers. Over the years, both at the gas pipeline company Transco and at the University of Warwick, in partnership with an external agency, I created a number of 360-degree instruments based on the organisation's own leadership competency framework. It's also possible to use a generic, off-the-shelf questionnaire and report.

Responses are usually gathered via an internet-based questionnaire, although some executive coaches will collect views through one-to-one interviews. A valuable aspect of 360-degree feedback is the comparison of the individual's own perspective with the views of others. Some 360-degree questionnaires include the opportunity to include textual answers to open questions. I find that the textual responses to open questions is often the most useful and thought-provoking part of the exercise for the client.

A possible downside of psychometric and 360-degree feedback tools – particularly if the results and report are well presented visually, which most are – is that it may create a spurious impression of accuracy. They are a classic illustration of the point that feedback needs to be digested, not swallowed whole.

In *Coaching Skills: A Handbook*, Jenny Rogers emphasises the importance of giving the client space to make their own sense of the feedback. She writes:

> *One of the most important questions in the debriefing discussion is, 'How does this seem to you?' or 'How does this tally with how you see yourself?' The client's answer here has to be the best and last word on the topic.*
>
> (Rogers, 2008)

In his chapter 'Using Psychometrics in Coaching', in the *Handbook of Coaching Psychology*, Alan Bourne writes:

> *The clients who gain the greatest benefit from psychometric tools are likely to be those who are open in their responses when completing them, open-minded and curious to understand themselves better and who do not take a defensive attitude to feedback which may challenge how they see themselves.*
>
> (Bourne, 2007)

In a coaching session, taking a client through their report or feedback hopefully raises their awareness. It's valuable to move on to helping them to think through what actions they will take in response. You might have time to do this within the session, or you may ask the client to do this afterwards. I like to give the client time to reflect upon and digest their feedback, and ask them to send me their considered thoughts later in answer to questions such as the following.

- What do you see as the main messages in your feedback?
- What goals will you set yourself as a result of this feedback?
- What steps will you take, and by when, to achieve each of these goals?

> **REFLECTIVE TASK**
>
> You can read more about the Insights Discovery Profile and how you might use it to help a client to understand their style, their strengths and the value they bring to their team on the company's website: www.insights.com/products/insights-discovery/
>
> The link includes some very quick, fun questions to get a sense of what might be your own colour preferences, and a short video introducing the instrument.
>
> To deepen your understanding, you might wish to become accredited through either a face-to-face or an online course. See: www.insights.com/insights-discovery-accreditation/
>
> I realise that I might be coming across as seeking to promote this particular instrument and organisation – that's not my intention. There are many other tools, instruments and profiles available.

## References

Bourne, A (2007) Using Psychometrics in Coaching. In Palmer, S and Whybrow, A (eds) *Handbook of Coaching Psychology* (pp 385–403). London: Routledge.

Insights (nd) What is Insights Discovery? [online] Available at: www.insights.com/products/insights-discovery/ (accessed 26 September 2022).

Passmore, J (ed) (2008) *Psychometrics in Coaching*. London: Kogan Page.

Rogers, J (2008) *Coaching Skills: A Handbook*. Maidenhead: McGraw Hill.

# Chapter 38: O

## OBJECTIVES, OBSTACLES, OPTIONS AND OUTCOMES

In choosing these four words as the focus for this chapter, I'm wondering if the OOOO model might become an alternative to the GROW model. (I'm not being serious!) It would stand for:

**O**bjectives    What are you trying to achieve?

**O**bstacles     What is getting in the way of you achieving these objectives?

**O**ptions       What might you do to pursue your objectives?

**O**utcomes      What insights or actions are you taking from this conversation?

Let's look at the four Os in turn.

### Objectives

The notion of objectives operates at several levels. First, there are the client's objectives for this particular conversation. Near the start of a coaching or a supervision session, I ask the client a question along the lines of *'What do you want to talk about today?'* I might follow this up with another question to clarify a more specific objective for the conversation by saying something like *'And if this is a really useful conversation, what would you like to be taking away?'*

Alongside objectives at the level of this particular conversation, the client will also have wider and longer-term objectives. This is akin to the G of the GROW model. *'What are you looking to achieve?'* *'What does success look like in regard to the issue you're exploring?'* In Chapter 34, 'Solution-focused coaching', we looked at the idea of asking what is known as the *miracle question*. This is along the lines of, *'If everything works out exactly as you would like, what would you be thinking, feeling and doing?'*

There is a commonly held notion that it's important to state objectives as SMART goals – aims need to be Specific, Measurable, Achievable, Relevant and Time-bound. While this can be useful, there may also be times when a client has a more general sense of where they want to head but aren't ready to specify exactly what they'll do by when. For the time being, their objectives are appropriately somewhat fuzzy.

## Obstacles

In some coaching conversations there may not be obstacles blocking the client in achieving their goals. The conversation might be about helping them, first, to clarify aims and, second, to choose actions to achieve these. However, there are other times when the client is very clear about what they want to achieve, and the key issue is helping them to work out how to overcome obstacles that are preventing them from taking steps to pursue their goals.

In the opening chapter we noted that sometimes we might need to modify the basic equation

$$\text{Awareness} + \text{responsibility} = \text{performance}$$

to read

$$\text{Awareness} + \text{responsibility} + \text{confidence} + \text{capability} = \text{performance}$$

I think that one of the toughest issues in coaching is when fear or a lack of confidence is preventing the client from taking action. This may go very deep, and the client might need to work with a counsellor or a therapist to explore and hopefully resolve what's blocking them. However, it may be possible within the appropriate boundaries of a coaching conversation to help a client to identify and overcome the barriers within themselves that are preventing them from taking action. In a later chapter, we'll discuss how a cognitive behavioural approach might be effective in helping the client to think and feel differently and hence to behave more effectively.

Another possibility that we also discussed in Chapter 34 on solution-focused coaching is to invite the client to recall times when they did act with confidence. They might be able to translate what they did then into a way forward in their current situation. In Chapter 22, 'Voicing', we discussed the idea of asking the client to give a name to their self who lacks confidence and another name to the self who is able to act confidently in some situations. You can then help them to explore how to bring their confident self to the fore to address their challenge.

## Options

The options phase is the same as in the O of the GROW model. The coach is helping the client to identify a number of possible options, from which they can choose the action steps that they want to commit to. There may be times when there is an obvious option where the client can see clearly what they will do. At other times, it may be helpful to explore a number of options before inviting the client to choose. A couple of questions from the silent coaching exercise that we looked at in the chapter on the GROW model may be useful in helping a client to identify some fresh options:

- If you had absolutely no constraints – of time or money or power or health – what would you do?
- If you had a really wise friend, what would they do in your shoes?

I also find that the simple question *'What else might you do?'* sometimes generates further possibilities for the client.

## Outcomes

Clients come to coaching for many different reasons. For example, some wish to perform more effectively in their role, some want to learn new skills or behaviours, some want to progress in their career, and others may be seeking to resolve conflict or enhance relationships. And so on. Some clients come because they have been *sent* by their organisation, who may have their own objectives for the coaching arrangement. The desired outcomes which clients are seeking can vary enormously. And sometimes the benefits they gain may be in areas that they wouldn't have identified at the outset of the coaching relationship.

Moreover, the problems and challenges facing clients come in different sizes. There may be times when there is a neat end to the conversation and the client has a clear action plan to go off and implement. However, there may also be times when they have got somewhere in terms of exploring the issue but don't yet know what they'll do – or maybe aren't yet ready to commit to an action.

A client will often think further about the conversation in the days, weeks and perhaps months afterwards. Sometimes the way forward might emerge for them as they reflect. This could be as a result of considered reflection, or it might be that clarity suddenly appears in a moment of insight. It doesn't matter whether or not the coach is present when this happens. We don't engage in coaching to get a round of applause at the end of the conversation!

**READING**

One of the other chapters I had in mind for the letter O was the OSKAR model. Like the GROW model, this is a framework for structuring a coaching session. The mnemonic stands for these five steps:

- Outcome
- Scaling
- Know-how
- Affirm and action
- Review (which takes place at the next session).

You can read more about the OSKAR framework at: https://worldofwork.io/2019/08/the-oskar-coaching-model/

The article includes this assessment:

*The OSKAR coaching model feels like a more consciously coaching oriented model than some other solution focused models. As with many models, it works by helping a coachee understand and bridge the gap between their current state and desired future state. It differs from some models though in that it focuses perhaps more on behaviors and ways of working than simply actions.*

# Chapter 39: N

## NEUROSCIENCE, THE SCARF MODEL AND THE CHIMP PARADOX

Neuroscience is the scientific study of the nervous system, including the brain. It is a fast-developing field, and is of increasing interest to practising coaches. In this chapter we briefly introduce neuroscience and its relevance for coaching before going on to discuss two topics that translate some key ideas from neuroscience into very accessible terms – the SCARF model and the Chimp Paradox.

In their chapter in *The Trainee Coach Handbook*, Sabine Schnell, Jonny Searle and Richard Stoneman write:

> *When we trust someone, they sense this and their brain releases oxytocin. This restricts the activity of the amygdala, the part of the brain responsible for emotion, thereby limiting their 'fight or flight' response. The absence of fear means their brain can function more effectively allowing them to think more creatively and logically. In fact, when we trust people, they are more likely to become more trustworthy.*

(Schnell et al, 2021)

An important aspect of neuroscience is the notion of neuroplasticity, which is the ability of neural networks in the brain to change, enabling the brain to be rewired to function differently. In their chapter in *Excellence in Coaching*, Carol Wilson and Frank Bresser write:

*Coaches help people to tap into this plasticity, firstly by helping them to identify their goals, and then by reinforcing the thoughts, ideas and actions which will take them to those goals.*

(Wilson and Bresser, 2021)

You can read much more about the brain and neuroscience, and applications to coaching, in Amy Brann's book *Neuroscience for Coaches: How Coaches and Managers Can Use the Latest Insights to Benefit Clients and Teams* (2022).

## The SCARF model

In an article entitled 'Managing with the Brain in Mind', David Rock (2008) draws on ideas from neuroscience to explore five factors that can activate a reward or threat response in our brain in social situations, including the workplace, educational settings and the family. The acronym SCARF refers to:

**S**tatus             Our relative importance to others.

**C**ertainty         Being able to predict the future.

**A**utonomy          Our sense of control over events.

**R**elatedness       A sense of safety with others, of friend rather than foe.

**F**airness          A perception of fair exchanges between people.

Status, certainty, autonomy, relatedness and fairness might be viewed as five values. Each of us will place a different importance on them. Moreover, what matters to us might shift over time. When we perceive that one of our important values is being threatened, then our initial reaction might be one of fight or flight.

Rock goes on to say:

> *If you are a leader, every action you take and every decision you make either supports or undermines the perceived levels of status, certainty, autonomy, relatedness, and fairness in your enterprise. In fact, this is why leading is so difficult. Your every word and glance is freighted with social meaning.*

(Rock, 2008)

The SCARF model is a useful guide for anyone managing change within an organisation. The individuals affected will be asking themselves what the change means for them personally. If you are coaching someone on the receiving end of organisational change, it's useful to explore what they feel they may be losing – and perhaps gaining. In terms of the SCARF model:

- some people may be worried that they're losing status;
- others may be anxious about the inevitable uncertainty created by the change;
- new reporting lines or systems many mean a loss of autonomy for some;
- others may be resistant because they will no longer be working with close colleagues or friends;
- an individual may be angry because they feel that they – or perhaps others – are being treated unfairly.

## The Chimp Paradox

In his best-selling book *The Chimp Paradox*, Steve Peters (2012) sets out a simplified model of the brain, replacing scientific names for parts of the brain with simple analogies.

He calls our prefrontal cortex the *Human* part of our brain. Our Human acts logically and rationally, basing decisions on facts. The Human enables us to thrive in modern society.

He calls our limbic system, the emotional centre of our brain, the *Inner Chimp*. The Chimp is the oldest part of our brain. It controls our fight, flight or freeze response, which was essential to keep our caveman ancestors alive when faced with genuine physical threats. The Chimp thinks short term and decides using emotions.

Peters calls a third aspect of our brain the *Computer*. This is spread throughout the brain, and stores information put into it by the Human or the Chimp. The Computer draws on this information to make fast and automatic responses. For example, once you've learnt how to ride a bike or make a cup of tea, your Computer enables you to do this repeatedly with very little conscious effort.

Our Chimp is designed to spot and deal with threats. In modern society, threats are everywhere – working for a rubbish boss, being cut up by a dangerous driver or encountering a rude shop assistant (or customer). The Chimp is an emotional machine that thinks independently from us. It is not good or bad, it is just a Chimp. We need to learn how to manage our Chimp.

Peters writes:

> One of the secrets of success and happiness is to learn to live with your Chimp and not get bitten or attacked by it. To do this, you need to understand how your Chimp behaves, and why it thinks and acts in the way that it does. You also need to understand your Human and not muddle up your Human with your Chimp.
>
> (Peters, 2012)

The idea of the Chimp Paradox is a metaphor that we can explore to help us to control our emotions, manage our responses, make wiser decisions, communicate more effectively and act in our best interests.

On the LeadershipPlus module of the full-time MBA at Warwick Business School we use an exercise to help students to get to know their Chimp and to consider how to manage it. You might use or modify the exercise for coaching a client or working with a team. We ask each student to spend five minutes reflecting on a time when their Chimp took over, what this felt like and how they behaved. We then invite them to take a sheet of flipchart paper and some coloured pens, and draw a picture that represents their Chimp. Artistic skill isn't important. They then make notes in answer to these questions:

- What are your Chimp's priorities?
- What triggers your Chimp?
- How does your Chimp behave?
- What name will you call your Chimp?

Each student then shares their picture and their thoughts with the other members of their syndicate. Giving a name to their Chimp sometimes acts as a handy shorthand reference point. The exercise also helps the students to understand each other a bit better, which can be invaluable for the work of the syndicate when tensions rise as assignment deadlines loom.

**REFLECTIVE TASK**

- Thinking of times when life and work is reasonably stable for you, which of the five factors in the SCARF model are most important for you? (You may choose more than one.)
- And, thinking of times of personal or organisational change that you personally have experienced, which of the five SCARF factors were most important for you? (You may choose more than one.)
- If these are different, what accounts for this?

My own answer to the first question is Fairness and Autonomy. My answer to the second question is Certainty.

# References

Brann, A (2022) *Neuroscience for Coaches: How Coaches and Managers Can Use the Latest Insights to Benefit Clients and Teams* (3rd edition). London: Kogan Page.

Peters, S (2012) *The Chimp Paradox*. London: Vermillion.

Rock, D (2008) Managing with the Brain in Mind. *NeuroLeadership Journal*, 1(1): 1–9.

Schnell, S, Searle, J and Stoneman, R (2021) The Coaching Relationship. In Watt, M, Bor, R and Florance, I (eds), *The Trainee Coach Handbook* (pp 27–46). London: Sage.

Wilson, C and Bresser, F (2021) What is Coaching? In Passmore, J (ed) *Excellence in Coaching* (4th edition, pp 13–33) London: Kogan Page.

# Chapter 40: M

## MEDIATION

In this chapter we explore how the skills and values of a primarily non-directive coaching approach can be used in mediation.

Just as coaching can be more or less directive, so too can mediation. In some forms of mediation, the person presiding may weigh the evidence and make a ruling that is binding on the parties. Or there may be a judge who will decide who is right and who is wrong, and who may impose a solution, a penalty or a punishment. These sit at the directive end of the spectrum.

However, we shall be focusing on a non-directive approach to mediation where the mediator isn't the person coming up with the solution, but rather is trying to help the participants to identify a way forward that will work for them. We'll look specifically at *workplace mediation* where the two parties who are in dispute are employees of the same organisation. They may well have to continue working with one another, so it's important that both feel that any agreement is satisfactory. The role of the mediator is to facilitate the conversation so that the participants together identify and agree what they are willing to commit to.

In *The Definitive Guide to Workplace Mediation and Managing Conflict at Work*, Clive Lewis offers a definition of mediation and notes some important features:

> *Mediation is a process used for resolving disputes in which a third person helps the parties negotiate a settlement. It is future focused and less concerned with who is right or wrong, and concentrates on solving problems so that*

*they don't occur again. The parties retain responsibility for achieving a solution.*

(Lewis, 2009)

As a mediator, you are seeking to establish a relationship of rapport and trust with both of the participants in the mediation. The nature of this relationship is similar to what you are trying to achieve with a coaching client. Carl Rogers' core conditions – empathic understanding, non-judgemental acceptance and being genuine – are fundamental in creating this type of relationship. So, too, is a sincere belief in the ability of people to find their own way forward. Moreover, the three conversational skills of a coach – listening to understand, asking mainly open questions that raise awareness and playing back your understanding – are vital in facilitating a mediation.

We explored a fourth conversational skill in Chapter 22; voicing is the ability to state clearly what you think and the reasons that underlie your thinking. In mediation, there may be differences between the participants in terms of status, confidence, assertiveness, emotional awareness or simply the ability to articulate their perspective. The mediator needs to be able to manage the conversation to give both parties sufficient air time to express their views. The mediator may have to be assertive to manage the conversation fairly, enabling both participants to voice their thoughts and feelings, their hopes and fears.

In carrying out a mediation, I follow a simple structure. Assuming that both parties are willing to engage in the mediation process (which is an important consideration), I have a separate initial meeting with each person, lasting between 60 and 90 minutes. The aims of these initial meetings are:

- to allow each party individually to talk through what's been happening, the impact on them and how they see the situation;

- to invite them to think about what they wish to happen going forwards;
- to begin to build a relationship of rapport and trust.

Most people only ever take part in mediation once in their lifetime, and generally feel anxious about what it will be like. Some dread the prospect of having to converse with the person they're in conflict with. Building rapport and trust with each party is very helpful. I reassure them that I am impartial, and often add that I'm *omnipartial* – I want both to get a good outcome.

I then have a meeting with both parties together. I usually allow four hours for this, although sometimes we don't need all of this time. The aims of the joint meeting are:

- to help each party to appreciate the other's perspective;
- to enable each party to state what they would like to happen going forwards;
- to seek to reach an agreement between both parties on what will happen going forwards.

I find that there are three generic outcomes. First, sometimes the two parties reach a *genuine agreement*. The joint session may well have been an emotional experience. Second, there may be a fairly superficial agreement, which strikes me as being very unlikely to make a real difference – I call this an *apparent agreement*. Third, sometimes *no agreement* is reached. I think that this is often better than an apparent agreement. It is worth noting that it can be the case that, although no agreement was reached, the experience of sharing important concerns was of value to one or both participants.

If agreement on a way forward is reached, I usually capture this shortly afterwards in an email. I send a draft to both parties to check for any amendments or omissions. If we end up *wordsmithing* the text over a period of weeks, this probably means that the process hasn't made a real difference. I also agree with the participants regarding what, if anything, will be shared with any third parties, such as their line manager or the HR business partner who commissioned the mediation. This might be as brief as a report that the mediation has taken place and an agreement has or hasn't been reached, without any detail whatsoever beyond this. However, the parties may wish to share more than this – it is their joint choice.

I usually offer to have a follow-up joint conversation with both to review progress some months later. I sometimes – but not always – offer each participant the option to contact me for a confidential one-to-one follow-up coaching conversation.

In his book *Relational Coaching*, Erik de Haan (2008) says that the most important factor affecting the outcome of coaching is the client. Similarly, I think the most important factor in whether or not a workplace mediation produces a meaningful agreement is the two participants – their willingness to listen to appreciate the other party's point of view; to say clearly what they feel, think and want; and their openness to the possibility that they themself might need to change.

Another thing I've learnt from doing mediation is that there is no single version of the truth. Both parties have very different perspectives. In Marian Roberts' book *Developing the Craft of Mediation* (2007), Lorraine Schaffer, a highly experienced mediator, says that, *'I think it took me two years of mediating before I stopped worrying about who was telling the truth and who wasn't. And really realising that there isn't a truth.'*

A mediation conversation feels more complex than a coaching conversation. Non-judgementally accepting both parties equally can be a challenge. The two participants may vary considerably in their level of emotional intelligence. Assessing where we're up to in the conversation can be difficult. Handling confidentiality can be tricky, too. Although I endeavour to check what I can share with the other party, I might inadvertently reveal a detail that I thought was unexceptional but which turns out to be significant.

On the other hand, the focus of a mediation is generally narrower than in coaching. The parties have come together to work through and resolve a particular issue or relationship. Moreover, a mediation intervention is likely to be fairly brief, perhaps over a single day, whereas a coaching relationship may last several years.

When mediation goes well – when the process enables the participants to move from confusion, anger and mistrust to understanding, acceptance and commitment – it feels a great privilege to be a mediator. This is another way in which mediation is similar to coaching

**READING**

ACAS, the Advisory, Conciliation and Arbitration Service, is an independent body that works with employers and employees to improve workplace relationships. One of the range of services offered by ACAS is mediation support. They offer advice to employers on how to set up a mediation scheme, train people to act as mediators and provide external mediators. The link below contains some practical advice on what mediation is and issues to consider: www. acas.org.uk/mediation

## References

de Haan, E (2008) *Relational Coaching: Journeys Towards Mastering One-to-One Learning*. Chichester: John Wiley.

Lewis, C (2009) *The Definitive Guide to Workplace Mediation and Managing Conflict at Work*. Weybridge: RoperPenberthy.

Roberts, M (2007) *Developing the Craft of Mediation*. London: Jessica Kingsley.

# Chapter 41: L

## COACHING AS A LINE MANAGER

In this chapter we shall explore how a line manager can use a coaching approach to manage their people. The idea of the directive to non-directive spectrum that we've mentioned in previous chapters is very relevant here. At the directive end of the spectrum, a coach or manager can give instructions, offer advice or guidance, and make suggestions. At the non-directive end they can listen to understand, ask genuinely open questions and play back their understanding in order to help the other person to explore their own ideas and come up with a solution.

Many managers operate exclusively at the directive end of the spectrum, issuing orders, giving instructions, telling people what to do. This is characteristic of a *Command and Control* approach to management. It may never have occurred to some that they could also move to the non-directive end to tap into the ideas, knowledge and creativity of the people who report to them.

There are extra challenges for a line manager that don't arise for an external coach or for an internal coach who isn't in the managerial line. One issue is confidentiality. An individual may well limit what they share with their boss, and find it easier to be honest with a coach. In *Coaching Skills: A Handbook*, Jenny Rogers writes:

> As a boss, it is entirely probable that you are part of whatever problems your coachee has and this can be difficult to see let alone acknowledge. Also, it is always more difficult to promise confidentiality, encourage or expect complete disclosure, set aside your own considerations or remain

*detached from the possible outcomes. As a boss you have a stake in the outcome, whereas when you are purely a coach you do not.*

(Rogers, 2008)

The final sentence highlights another challenge around objectives. An independent coach doesn't have an agenda of their own, and can focus on the objectives of the client – although they may also take into account the needs of the organisation. However, a line manager has specific objectives that are central to their role. These often have been passed down from further up the organisation. In seeking to achieve results through the efforts of their people, the line manager must balance their own objectives and the goals of the organisation with the aspirations of those who report to them. This is a crucial consideration.

A useful model to handle this tension is the idea of the *coaching dance.* There are, legitimately, many occasions when the manager simply has to *tell* an individual what they need to do. And there are times when they can usefully *ask* people for their views and ideas. The manager needs to be able to dance skilfully between *telling* and *asking*. To give a simple illustration, a manager might say to one of their team:

- I must have the report by 3.00 on Friday. *(Tell)*
- What do you need to do to complete it by then? And what help do you need? *(Ask)*

The idea of skilfully dancing between telling and asking can also be used to think about feedback, motivation and development.

In Chapter 6, 'Feedback', we highlighted the difference between *giving* and *generating* feedback. The former is about the manager telling the individual what they thought about their performance, while the latter is about first asking the individual what they themselves thought they did well and less well.

In terms of motivation, a manager may have a range of carrots or sticks that they can hand out to reward or punish people. On the other hand, they might seek to understand what the individual finds rewarding and motivating, building this into their objectives if this is feasible. Giving people appropriate freedom to tackle an assignment in their own way is likely to be more motivating than micro-managing them.

Moreover, tackling a job with creativity and a degree of freedom will also help to build the individual's skills and confidence. A coaching approach, in contrast to a Command and Control approach, is much more likely to develop people.

Some managers object that they don't have time to use a coaching approach. It is usually quicker to give a command, and there may be occasions when there genuinely isn't time to coach. However, taking time to delegate a task can be an investment. By building the capability of their people, the manager can free up their own schedule to tackle more strategic work – or have a better work–life balance.

One occasion that lends itself well to a coaching approach is a performance and development review, which happens in many organisations. This is often an annual ritual that is more about filling in and filing forms than it is about enhancing performance or developing people. However, it can be an invaluable opportunity for a meaningful conversation that establishes clear objectives, identifies relevant development opportunities and builds trust and rapport in the relationship. Asking some open questions and listening to understand the answers is a much more valuable use of time than completing paperwork.

One situation where a coaching approach may not be appropriate is when an individual has been underperforming or behaving inappropriately for some time. There may be a variety of reasons for this. If the manager has explored these, and given the individual an opportunity to raise their game without success, it may become necessary to invoke a formal performance management procedure. And there are occasions when it's necessary to dismiss the individual. Coaching is a valuable part of the manager's toolkit, but it's not the whole story!

The idea of asking questions, listening to the answers and playing back what was said can extend also to how the manager engages with their team collectively. For example, in terms of making decisions, there is again a spectrum of possibilities. In some situations it may be entirely appropriate for the manager simply to announce the decision. In others, they may consult the team, take into account their views and let these inform the decision that the manager makes. Or, the manager may facilitate a discussion which not only explores perspectives but also reaches a collective decision on the way forward that everyone is committed to.

Using the coaching dance with individuals and sharing appropriately decision-making may shape the culture, or subculture, within a team. However, it is very difficult to create a subculture of empowerment and trust, say, within a team when the wider culture of the organisation is one of micro-management and a lack of trust. Culture generally flows from the top of an organisation – it is a vital responsibility of leadership.

**READING**

Some years ago I wrote a book called *The Coaching Dance* (Thomson, 2012) in which I set out some of the key ideas on coaching through the medium of a fictional story. The blurb on the back cover reads:

*Disillusioned with his job in the City, idealistic Ben Lindsay joins Hathaway Publishing International, where he manages a team of people for the first time. After some early disastrous meetings, Ben works with a coach who helps him to develop his own coaching skills, which Ben deploys to manage effectively and with integrity. The story conveys the basics of coaching and its use in managing people through the experiences of a novice manager.*

You can find the book on Amazon via this link: www.amazon.co.uk/Coaching-Dance-tale-coaching-management/dp/1478232145

## References

Rogers, J (2008) *Coaching Skills: A Handbook*. Maidenhead: McGraw Hill.

Thomson, B (2012) *The Coaching Dance*. Winchester: Docuracy.

# Chapter 42: K

## KANTOR'S FRAMEWORKS

In his book *Reading the Room: Group Dynamics for Coaches and Leaders*, David Kantor (2012) sets out a theory, which he calls Structural Dynamics, that explains *'how face-to-face communication works and does not work in human systems'*. He writes:

> *The title of this book refers to a priceless leadership skill: the ability to read the room to understand what's going on as people communicate in small groups, including how the leader himself or herself is participating, when the conversation is moving forward, when it may be just about to leave the rails, and possibly even how to guide it back on course.*

(Kantor, 2012)

Kantor sets out three communication models that combine together in his overall theory. I think that each of these models on its own is a useful framework to help someone to make sense of both their own communication preferences and also of the dynamics within the team that they are a member of or lead. As a coach, you might use one or more of the models when coaching an individual or – perhaps even more powerfully – when working with a team. We look at two of Kantor's three models, and mention briefly the third.

### The four-player system

Kantor states that there are only four basic vocal acts in a conversation. These are shown in Figure 42.1.

**Figure 42.1  Kantor's four-player system**

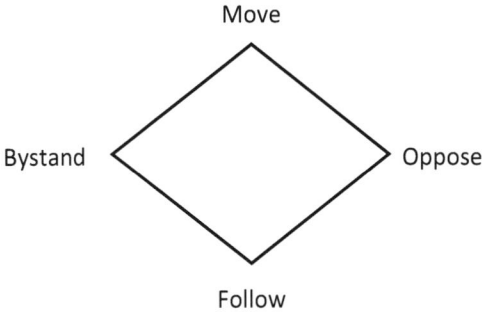

- When someone *moves*, they are proposing something or initiating an action.
- When someone *follows*, they are supporting a move.
- When someone *opposes*, they are challenging what is being said or proposed.
- When someone *bystands*, they are offering a perspective on what is happening in the conversation. They may be attempting to reconcile competing actions. (Note the term *bystanding* does not mean being uninvolved or silent.)

Here is a simple illustration. Imagine that a group of friends are discussing what to do this evening.

- Move: *Let's go to the cinema.*
- Follow: *There's a really good film on at the Odeon.*
- Oppose: *I'd rather have dinner together this evening.*
- Bystand: *We've spent an hour talking about what we might do this evening without reaching a decision.*

A healthy and constructive conversation requires all of these roles to be played. To make progress, someone has to offer an idea or a proposal. It's also useful for an initial suggestion to be developed and fleshed out. There may be times when the initial suggestion isn't ideal or workable, so it's vital that there is freedom within the group for ideas to be challenged and alternatives offered. In the words of the French philosopher Émile Chartier: '*Nothing is more dangerous than an idea when it is the only one you have.*'

And, in a highly functioning team, it's valuable to spend some time reflecting on the process of the group – what's working and what's not working. Many groups literally never reflect on how the group is functioning.

If you are coaching a team, then it's worth exploring which individuals tend to play which roles, to discuss which of the roles is lacking in their conversations, and to agree changes that will enhance the quality of conversation and decision-making in the group.

## Three languages

A second part of Kantor's theory is the idea that each of us speaks in one of three preferred languages. We tend to be interested in and hence to pay more attention to one of three *'domains'*. In Kantor's terminology:

- People who speak the language of *power* focus on making decisions and agreeing actions.
- Some individuals speak the language of *meaning* and attend to ideas and ways of understanding.
- Those who speak the language of *affect* concentrate on feelings and on connections between people.

When I worked in the gas pipeline company Transco, our engineers spoke the language of power. They were keen to make decisions and get into action. At workshops, they were less interested in reflecting on and making sense of events.

Moving to the University of Warwick, I found, not unexpectedly, that academics spoke the language of meaning. When a colleague ran workshops to introduce a new performance and development review process, she received many challenges from academics who were more interested in disputing the philosophy behind the process than in actually doing a review.

I don't have a clear example from my own experience of a group who spoke the language of affect, but one might imagine that a team of counsellors would tend to speak that language.

Those who speak the language of meaning or of affect find it much more difficult to address the question *'What are we going to do?'* If the purpose of a meeting is to make a decision, then someone needs at the appropriate time to focus everyone's attention on this.

I want to suggest that there may be a fourth language, which I'll call the language of *bureaucracy*. For example, the culture of a university necessarily has to reflect policies and procedures that are designed appropriately to produce consistency and to be fair to all of the students. There may, however, be times when this is taken too far – following procedures to the letter can get in the way of making common-sense decisions. As an illustration from a different context, in the early days of the war in Ukraine when thousands of people were fleeing, the UK authorities insisted that biometrically validated visa applications had to be in order before a refugee was allowed into Britain. I don't think that someone who spoke the language of power or of affect would have taken such a stance.

## Operating system

Kantor states that there are three types of operating system – open, closed and random – which reflect the basic rules that are followed when people interact with one another. Each of these has advantages and limitations.

- In an *open system*, people feel free to offer dissenting views and to speak candidly. Learning and adaptation through participation are valued. Authority and power are shared.
- In a *closed system*, there is an emphasis on order and rules, predictability and efficiency. Tradition and legacy are valued. People defer to those in power for decisions.
- In a *random system*, there is innovation, autonomy and freedom. Individuals are encouraged to *do their own thing*. Authority and power are shared.

A university may well combine a closed-system administration overseeing an open-system or random-system set of academics!

**REFLECTIVE TASK**

I believe that my own natural preference is the language of meaning. I studied maths as an undergraduate, and was more interested in pure maths than in applied maths. Working in organisations for many years, I think I've developed some fluency in the language of power – I'm often keen to get things done rather than debate endlessly. In a coaching or mediation context, I need to be able to attend to the language of affect. I believe that I can do this reasonably well, but it's not my 'native tongue'.

Think about the language that you yourself tend to speak in and pay attention to. Place an X in the triangle below to reflect the balance of where you operate. This might be different in a work context than in your life outside work.

**Figure 42.2 Kantor's three languages**

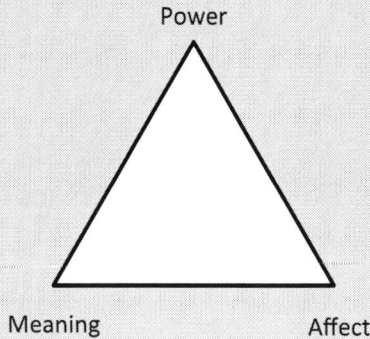

Power

Meaning          Affect

Make some notes on what you might do differently to contribute more effectively to meetings or conversations.

## Reference

Kantor, D (2012) *Reading the Room: Group Dynamics for Coaches and Leaders*. San Francisco, CA: Jossey-Bass.

# Chapter 43: J

## THE CLIENT'S JOURNEY

The word *coach*, in the sense that we're exploring, was first used in the nineteenth century to refer to someone who tutored a student to carry them through the entrance exams for the University of Oxford. It derives from the name of a small Hungarian town, Kocs, where a popular type of horse-drawn carriage was built. There is a sense, then, that coaching is about taking a client on a journey. In Chapter 29, 'Exploring metaphors', we noted metaphors such as *tour guide*, *mountain guide* or *travelling companion* for the role of a coach.

The coach accompanies the client on their journey, offering a range of support to assist them as they travel. But the destination of the journey is set by the client.

In this chapter we look at the journey a coaching client might experience as they contemplate signing up for coaching, engage in a series of coaching conversations and assimilate the insights and learnings they gained into their work and life after the coaching relationship ends. Before, during and after.

### Before

There are a number of routes that might take a client into coaching. Some will be thinking of their future career, either which path to choose or how to advance within their chosen profession. Some will have become aware of problems, challenges or worries, and want to be helped to resolve these. And some will be looking to develop new skills and behaviours.

There are two other routes into coaching which may be more problematic. Some people might come for coaching because someone else, maybe their boss or HR business partner, recommends it. They may be more or less clear why they're signing up, and some might not actually wish to be coached. They may be compliant rather than committed. Others may be taking part in a more general management development programme that includes some coaching sessions as part of a portfolio of activities. Again, some of them might not actually want to be coached.

Depending on how well they understand the coaching process, and also on the nature of the issues that have led them to coaching, clients may be anxious as they anticipate their first session. They may not know what to expect – or what is expected of them. As someone once said, '*You don't know what milk tastes like till you've tasted milk!*'

## During

The first coaching session might be what is termed a *chemistry session*, giving the client the opportunity to decide if they want to be coached by this particular coach. There may also be occasions when the coach decides to turn down the assignment. A key task for the coach in an opening session is to provide some reassurance to the client that they are entering a safe space where they will be treated professionally, respectfully and, I hope, non-judgementally by the coach. This is the start of the process of building rapport and trust in the relationship.

The client has a number of responsibilities if they wish to get the most from their coaching sessions.

- They need to be open and honest, sharing what really matters to them, what their hopes and aspirations are, and what they are unsure of or perhaps afraid of. This openness may well grow and deepen over time as trust and rapport build. The client may tell the coach things in the fourth session that they weren't ready to share in the first conversation.

- They need to think and reflect hard during the sessions. They also need to be willing to engage in exercises that the coach might propose, such as reflective writing or taking a psychometric test.
- They also need to do the work that's required between sessions. They may have agreed to experiment with some behaviours, and reflect on their experience. For example, they may have agreed to have a challenging conversation with their boss, or to make changes in how they spend their time. The coach may have given them material on ideas and models to read and assimilate.
- They also need to prepare for the next session, including being clear what they want to discuss.

The coach and client share a responsibility for the success of the sessions. The client may need to raise concerns with the coach if they are dissatisfied with progress. And they might sometimes have to terminate the sessions, possibly going on to work with a different coach.

## After

Coaching often, but not always, works. Clients clarify goals, make and carry out action plans, and learn new ways of thinking. The impact of a good coaching experience doesn't end at the last conversation. The client may continue to draw upon their learning for years to come. And there may be insights that take time to emerge, perhaps in an *ah ha!* moment when things fall into place and the client has a fresh view of some part of their world.

While I was drafting this chapter, a former client, whom I last worked with about ten years ago, sent me an email asking if we could have a one-off session to help him to defuse an issue that had arisen at work and which was causing him considerable distress. I was very pleased to do so. It was great to hear that years later he still appreciated the value of our sessions and relationship.

We said earlier that the coach accompanies the client on their journey. When it works well, the client is enabled to become their own guide, able to travel far without any further input from the coach. And able to help other people on their journeys, too.

---

**REFLECTIVE TASK**

In this chapter we have considered the journey that a client takes. As a coach, you yourself are also on a journey. In his book *The Coaching Relationship in Practice* Geoff Pelham addresses the reader about their journey to learn how to become a coach:

> *It is a journey of personal and professional development, and it is very likely that on your own journey you too will make some important decisions about your life and its future direction. Coaching has that effect.*
>
> (Pelham, 2016)

On the final page of the book he writes:

> *The metaphor and images of path and journey really capture for me the essence of coaching: both learning about it and working with coachees.*
>
> (Pelham, 2016)

Here is an exercise to reflect upon your own journey of development as a coach.

- Take a large piece of paper and draw a line that represents your journey. Mark and label those events which you regard as significant experiences in your learning and practice.
- For each of these events, add some further notes which capture what was important, satisfying or challenging about them for you.
- Extend the line into the future. Which places do you particularly want to visit on your coaching journey?

## Reference

Pelham, G (2016) *The Coaching Relationship in Practice*. London: Sage.

# Chapter 44: I

## IMPOSTOR SYNDROME

I recall an executive coach telling me that an issue she frequently encountered in coaching chief executives was their fear that, now they were at the top of their organisation, they were about to be found out as some kind of fraud. In their book *The Coach's Casebook*, Geoff Watts and Kim Morgan (2015) explore 12 issues that clients regularly bring to coaching. The first chapter focuses on impostor syndrome, a condition which seems to affect many people – including chief executives – at some point.

Note that the term *syndrome* may be misleading. The American Psychiatric Association's *Diagnostic and Statistical Manual of Mental Disorders* does not include impostor syndrome in its lengthy list of mental illnesses.

Watts and Morgan open their chapter with this quote from the psychotherapist Nathaniel Branden who explored the psychology of self-esteem:

> *Of all the judgements we pass in life, none is more important than the judgement we pass on ourselves.*
>
> (quoted in Watts and Morgan, 2015)

They go on to describe these classic symptoms of impostor syndrome.

- Having an inability to internalise your accomplishments.
- Feeling that other people have an overinflated view of you.

- Attributing any success that you have to luck or just being in the right place at the right time.
- Being fearful of being 'found out'.
- Feeling like a fraud.
- Believing that the very fact that you got the job/do this work means that it can't be that difficult. Your ability to do something negates the very value of it.
- Looking more at what you can't do, rather than valuing what you can do.

There are a number of possible issues that may underlie someone's feelings of being an impostor. They might be a perfectionist or suffer from other self-limiting beliefs. They may have a great fear of failure. They may have a very strong *inner critic* – a harsh, judgemental, critical inner voice. They may have a lack of confidence.

People who suffer from impostor syndrome are often driven to achieve more and more, and may appear to others to be very successful in their career – but their achievements don't alleviate the condition. Life or work can be highly stressful for them.

As a coach, it is important to work within appropriate boundaries. Some clients may simply be taking time to master a new and larger job, and the term *impostor syndrome* may be overstating things. For others, the struggle they bring to coaching may be part of a deeper and central aspect of their personality. While recognising that the client may have psychological issues which they might appropriately address with a counsellor or therapist, it is possible to draw upon ideas from, for example, cognitive behavioural coaching or solution-focused coaching to help a client to manage themself more effectively and to lessen the negative feelings they experience. Here are three possibilities.

One idea, which we'll discuss in Chapter 50, 'Cognitive behavioural coaching', is the ABCDE model.

- **A**ctivating event.

- **B**eliefs and perceptions about this event.

- **C**onsequences – cognitive, emotional, behavioural, physical or interpersonal.

- **D**isputing of self-limiting beliefs.

- **E**ffective and new ways of thinking and behaving.

You might work with the client to dispute (D) the internal thoughts or irrational or self-limiting beliefs (B) which underpin their impostor syndrome, helping them to identify and apply more helpful ways of thinking.

A second option is based on the idea that each of us is a *community of selves*, which Robert Hobson (1985) explores in his book *Forms of Feeling: The Heart of Psychotherapy*. He suggests that each of us has a number of sub-personalities or selves. I worked with this idea in a coaching session that was recorded for use as part of an online resource to accompany the book *Advanced Coaching Practice* by Christian van Nieuwerburgh and David Love (2019). I had a 40-minute, one-off coaching conversation with a client called Lina. The issue that Lina brought to the session was her impostor syndrome that she experienced at work. I helped Lina to identify two selves, which she named *Cool and Collected Lina* and *Hot Mess Lina*. I then asked Lina to do some reflective writing to explore how she might draw upon *Cool and Collected Lina* to manage her thoughts, feeling and actions when she felt *Hot Mess Lina* triggering her impostor syndrome.

Regarding a third option, Watts and Morgan (2015) describe a number of techniques *'aimed at helping clients acknowledge their qualities and achievements in order to give themselves more credit'*. They call one of these the *magazine interview*:

> *Ask your client to imagine that they have been interviewed by a magazine of their choice. Encourage your client to view themselves through the eyes of the interviewer, who wants to show your client in the best possible light, showcasing all of their skills, career highlights and qualities in order to inspire their readers.*

> *Ask you client to write the interview in the third person, including some photographs, and to bring it to the next session. It is even more powerful if they are prepared to read it out to you.*

> (Watts and Morgan, 2015)

Impostor syndrome is also a condition that can afflict coaches. In his book *The Coaching Relationship in Practice*, Geoff Pelham (2016) discusses how this might affect someone who is stepping up from training to be a coach to someone who is actually working as a coach, either independently or within an organisation. Hopefully, this is a temporary phenomenon as the new coach begins to embrace an identity as a coach rather than someone who is learning how to coach. There comes a point in your journey of development as a coach when it's useful to declare – to yourself – that you are a coach. In her book *The Coaching Manual*, Julie Starr highlights the importance of having the sense that part of your identity is being a coach:

> *When you have the inner sense of alignment that comes with being a coach, your confidence, your surety and your energy will all flow more naturally.*

> (Starr, 2011)

**VIDEO**

In this eight-minute TED talk Meredith Peebles explores her own impostor syndrome. She sets out in a very engaging way how she has chosen to empower herself to:

- own what she looks like;
- own what she does;
- own what she wants.

www.youtube.com/watch?v=lo65fyW1Xy0

## References

Hobson, R (1985) *Forms of Feeling: The Heart of Psychotherapy*. London: Tavistock Publications.

Pelham, G (2016) *The Coaching Relationship in Practice*. London: Sage.

Starr, J (2011) *The Coaching Manual*. Harlow: Pearson.

van Nieuwerburgh, C and Love, D (2019) *Advanced Coaching Practice*. London: Sage.

Watts, G and Morgan, K (2015) *The Coach's Casebook*. Cheltenham: Inspect and Adapt.

# Chapter 45: H

## HOW NOT TO COACH

In Chapter 8, '*How to coach*', I set out my definition of coaching that is the foundation of my approach:

*Coaching is a relationship of rapport and trust in which the coach uses their ability to listen, to ask questions and to play back what the client has communicated in order to help the client to clarify what matters to them and to work out what to do to achieve their aspirations.*

One way of understanding *How not to coach* is to do the opposite of the key points in the definition.

On the Warwick Business School Distance Learning MBA module on leadership we share a four-minute video demonstrating how not to coach. We made the video with two actors playing an ineffective male manager and a female employee who has approached him with some concerns. You can watch the video via this link: www.dropbox.com/s/lacsszvqbl1t6zy/Line%20Manager-poor%20coaching.mp4?dl=0. We ask the students to note at least ten things the manager does that are unhelpful – they find it all too easy to spot at least ten! Their posts include observations such as the following.

- Fiddles with his phone and notebook, doesn't make eye contact, distracted.
- Body language suggests he's not interested. Doesn't pick up on her body language either.
- Appears uninterested. No sign of empathy.

- Doesn't listen.
- Interrupts. Doesn't allow her to speak freely.
- Doesn't acknowledge that there are issues troubling her.
- Answers his own questions. Makes assumptions. Jumps to conclusions.
- Manipulates the conversation. Offers trite solutions. Makes vague statements without any substance.
- Patronises. Dismisses or trivialises concerns. Suggests her concerns are unimportant.
- Complete lack of structure in the conversation.

One student added, '*He really loves the sound of his own voice.*'

On their website the Center for Executive Coaching have an article called '18 Examples of Bad Coaching Habits'. Here are 18 things not to do as a coach, together with some comments from the website.

### One: Fixing

*The problem with fixing the client's problem is that just because you know the answer and would be able to implement it doesn't mean your client can.*

### Two: Knowing the answer and manipulating

*Don't play the game called 'What's in my pocket?' If you already know the answer you want the person to also know, and you are not flexible about it, don't torture them. Simply tell them.*

### Three: Interrupting

*Don't interrupt when you coach. This deceptively simple rule can be hard for coaches who process information quickly.*

### Four: Distracted coaching

*If you are in a noisy place, have crises to handle, are on the phone, or checking your email on your laptop, you are not in a position to coach.*

### Five: Stacking questions

*Stacking questions means that you ask your client more than one question at a time. Be patient. Let the process unfold. Ask one question at a time. If you do, you might also find that the next logical question is different from what you had expected.*

### Six: Checklist coaching

*Checklist coaching means that you already have a list of questions to ask. There is no need to listen and no room for creativity or flexibility.*

### Seven: The diagnostic

*'Have you tried A? Have you tried B? Have you tried C? Have you tried D?'*

*It's similar to having an algorithm or flow chart and similar to a doctor trying to diagnose a disease.*

### Eight: Hiding suggestions

*Some coaches hide their ideas in the form of a question, thinking that asking any type of question is good coaching. 'Have you tried X?'*

### Nine: Bringing up some sort of fad book or trend

*Some coaches are suckers for the latest trend or fad.*

### Ten: Never-ending, open-ended questions

*Some coaches believe you can never offer advice or observations to a client. They insist on only asking open-ended questions. As a result, their coaching feels more like therapy. It also becomes frustrating.*

### Eleven: Caring more than they do and getting frustrated

*Sometimes it feels that you care more about the client's goals and aspirations than the client does.*

*If you start judging the client, become exasperated, or even chide them during coaching sessions, you have jumped into the realm of bad coaching.*

### Twelve: Getting trained on the client's time

*If you find you are asking clients to bring you up to speed on key terminology, how to do their job, or in-depth play-by-play about what happened recently, you might be doing things that are valuable to you but meaningless to the client.*

### Thirteen: Doing the client's dirty work

*Coaching isn't about stepping in and doing a client's work. It is about helping clients be more effective so that they can do the work without you.*

### Fourteen: Failing to put in place ways to track progress and measure results.

*If you neglect to agree on a clear intent and outcome with your client, you won't know if you achieve results.*

### Fifteen: Piling too much homework on your clients.

*The best homework is not homework at all, but rather application of new insights that helps the client improve performance and that fits naturally into what they have to do anyway.*

### Sixteen: Blaming the client when they don't participate fully in your coaching.

*If the client isn't participating or doesn't seem coach-able, has it occurred to you that it might be because of your coaching style or approach?*

### Seventeen: Dead air during coaching sessions.

*If you don't know what to ask during a coaching session, at a minimum, ask the client what they want to focus on.*

### Eighteen: Being a therapist instead of a coach.

*It can be challenging to recognize the temptation to step into unintentional therapy.*

(Center for Executive Coaching, nd)

In his book *Effective Coaching*, Myles Downey offers these words on the role of the coach:

*The primary function of the coach is to understand, not to solve, fix, heal, make better or be wise – to understand. The magic is that it is in that moment of understanding that the coachees themselves understand for themselves, become more aware and are then in a position to make better decisions and choices than they would have done anyway. That is how coaching is profoundly simple and simply profound. But most of us struggle to get above our own agenda and want to be seen to be making a difference.*

(Downey, 2003)

I love this quote. For me, it gets to the heart of what coaching is – and isn't! As a coach, your role isn't to *'solve, fix, heal, make better or be wise'*!

> **VIDEO**
>
> This seven-minute video discusses ten coaching mistakes, and offers ideas on what to do instead: www.youtube.com/watch?v=MV0hAmtF1EA
>
> I have reservations about a couple of the points made. For example, I'm not sure that as a coach you always need to share your intuition. We discussed this in Chapter 32, 'Use of self'. And I don't think that all coaching conversations need to finish with a commitment – sometimes the client isn't ready to commit at the end of a session.

## References

Center for Executive Coaching (nd) 18 Examples of Bad Coaching Habits. [online] Available at: https://centerforexecutivecoaching.com/bad-coaching-habits/ (accessed 26 September 2022).

Downey, M (2003) *Effective Coaching: Lessons from the Coach's Coach*. London: Texere.

# Chapter 46: G

## GESTALT COACHING

Like a number of other approaches, Gestalt coaching evolved from therapy and counselling. The German word *Gestalt* has no exact equivalent in English. It embraces notions such as shape, form, configuration, pattern, whole. To form a Gestalt is to complete a pattern.

In their chapter in the *Handbook of Coaching Psychology*, Julie Allan and Alison Whybrow (2007) write that, '*Gestalt coaching concerns a process of becoming fully aware and turning that awareness into action.*' The coach assists the client to deepen their awareness of their whole self – their thoughts and feelings, their patterns of behaviour, and their physiological reactions.

There are three philosophical principles that are fundamental to Gestalt therapy, counselling and coaching – phenomenology, field theory and dialogue. Let's look at these in turn.

### Phenomenology

Phenomenology is concerned with the study of objects and events as we perceive them. It seeks to distinguish between what is actually being perceived in the here-and-now and what is a residue from past experiences. A client's behaviour within a coaching session will reflect how they behave more generally in the world, and hence a Gestalt coach may draw the client's attention to what is happening *in the moment* during a conversation. The coach might describe what they observe or share what they notice within themself. But they will avoid interpreting or diagnosing.

## Field theory

Each of us exists within a wider context or *field*, and we understand ourself in relation to that field. What we notice – what stands out for us in any situation – reflects our past experiences, our current thoughts and feelings, and our hopes and fears for the future. A key idea is the notion of *figure and ground.* As an illustration, what you see in the image in Figure 46.1 below may be either a candlestick or two faces. When one is figure, the other is background.

**Figure 46.1  A candlestick or two faces?**

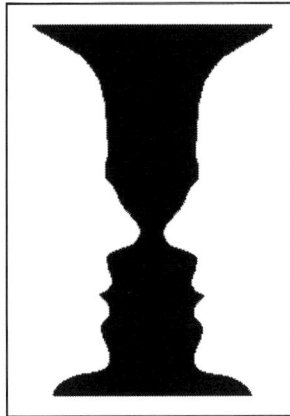

A Gestalt coach helps the client to become fully aware of figure and ground. Different figures may emerge for the client from the wider ground or context as a coaching session unfolds. An important consideration is that the coach is inevitably part of the client's field, which underlines the importance of the coach–client relationship.

## Dialogue

The philosopher Martin Buber distinguished between *I–Thou* interactions in which two people engage with each other in open, mutually respectful ways without seeking to impose their will on the other person, and *I–It* interactions where one or both parties treat the other as some kind of object to be shaped or manipulated. Much everyday conversation is – appropriately – of the *I–It* variety. In his article 'The Relational Attitude in Gestalt Therapy Theory and Practice', Gary Yontef notes that:

> *Dialogue in therapy means that the therapist works on the therapeutic task by contacting the patient as the patient is, the whole person that the patient is, with the whole person of the therapist him or herself. A whole person includes being flawed and allowing that flaw to be a recognized part of one's existence, even in the therapeutic setting with patients.*
>
> (Yontef, 2002)

As we noted, a Gestalt coach aims to help the client to be fully aware and to be fully present, tuning into what is most important for them at that moment. Allan and Whybrow (2007) write that:

> *The process of Gestalt coaching is to work to sharpen individual experience, to become aware of our assumptions and stereotypes and to challenge them in order to see what is taking place more clearly and therefore respond to what is actually happening, not what we think is happening.*

This sharpened awareness thus helps the client to respond differently. Encouraging the client to reflect upon their patterns of behaviour helps them to make changes in their behaviour. Gestalt coaching takes the existential view that each individual is responsible for their own decisions and actions – or indecisions and inactions. The Gestalt approach reflects the basic proposition that we discussed in the opening chapter:

Awareness + responsibility = performance

Another notion in Gestalt is the paradoxical theory of change. In her chapter 'The Gestalt Supervision Model', Marion Gillie writes that paradoxically

> *change occurs when one becomes what one is, not when he tries to become what he is not ... one must stand in one place in order to have a firm footing to move ... once*

*a person can stand* fully *in the place that is reality, then the energy that gets diverted into rebellion is released and mobilized towards something which is a genuine choice.*

(Gillie, 2011, emphasis original)

Thus a full awareness of what *is* becomes necessary for genuine choice and lasting change to occur. Paradoxically, acknowledging one's actual state and existence supports personal growth and change.

Gestalt uses the notion of *unfinished business* to describe a situation when we are unable to obtain *closure*. Unfinished business reflects an incomplete Gestalt. This may reflect a current need – maybe we are hungry and unable to eat just now. Or it may reflect experiences from the past – for example, the needs we had as infants that weren't satisfactorily met, or a bereavement that we haven't fully come to terms with, or the bullying we experienced at school but did not talk about. This kind of unfinished business and inability to obtain closure consumes psychological and emotional energy.

As well as working in the here-and-now, a Gestalt coach may also use *experiments* in their work with a client, encouraging the client to try out new thoughts or actions within the safety of the coaching relationship.

One example of experimenting is the *empty chair* exercise. I use the exercise when a client is speaking a lot about another person, maybe their manager or someone from their past. I invite the client to sit in a different chair, to imagine that they *are* the other person, and to answer some relevant questions as if they were that other person – using *I* rather than *he* or *she*. I might invite the client to return to their own chair and respond to what's just been said. There may be several rounds of 'conversation' between the client and the other person. I often finish by inviting the client to stand up and look down upon the two chairs, asking them what they've noticed about what is going on between the two parties or the nature of the relationship between them.

The empty chair exercise can be a powerful and emotional experience for a client. In using such an exercise, it's important to gain the client's consent, to be sensitive to their needs and concerns, and not to stray into therapeutic territory.

The *relationship* between client and coach is vitally important in Gestalt. We noted earlier that Gestalt coaching is based on an authentic *I–Thou* dialogue between the two participants. The coach brings their self and their presence to the relationship. In Chapter 32, 'Use of self', we noted these words of Marion Gillie:

> *Presence ... includes how 'grounded' you are in yourself and your work, how able you are to 'contact' the client, even when they are difficult to reach. It is the ability to be in the here and now, ie to tune into what is going on within yourself ... as you are impacted by them, and to disclose some of this in order to make contact.*

(Gillie, 2021)

**VIDEO**

This video describes another key idea in a Gestalt approach – the *cycle of experience*. It also discusses different *blocks* that get in the way of completing a cycle satisfactorily, creating some form of *unfinished business*. Although the video is less than five minutes long, it touches on a large number of ideas: www.youtube.com/watch?v=GZyF0JsyreM

## References

Allan, J and Whybrow, A (2007) Gestalt Coaching. In Palmer, S and Whybrow, A (eds) *Handbook of Coaching Psychology* (pp 133–59). London: Routledge.

Gillie, M (2011) The Gestalt Supervision Model. In Passmore, J (ed) *Supervision in Coaching* (pp 45–63). London: Kogan Page.

Yontef, G (2002) The Relational Attitude in Gestalt Therapy Theory and Practice. *International Gestalt Journal*, 25(1): 15–34.

# Chapter 47: F

## FACILITATION AND SOCRATIC QUESTIONING

The *Cambridge Business English Dictionary* defines facilitation as:

*the act of helping other people to deal with a process or reach an agreement or solution without getting directly involved in the process, discussion, etc. yourself.*

As an academic at Warwick Business School, I regard my role as a facilitator of learning, not a teacher. I'm not being pedantic here – I think there's a crucial difference. And I suspect that many of my colleagues would view their role differently from me.

My approach to teaching and learning (a neat phrase that perhaps glosses over the differences between the two activities) rests on two foundations. One is a primarily non-directive approach, based on the ideas of Carl Rogers, which also underpins my work as a coach. And the other is the power of experiential learning, which we explored in Chapter 11 on the Kolb learning cycle, where I wrote that:

*Deep and sustained learning – becoming able to do something you couldn't do before – only comes through experience. However, experience on its own isn't enough. In order to learn, we need to reflect upon and make sense of our experience.*

I regard my role as a facilitator as being to enable people to reflect upon and learn from their experiences. These might be previous experiences from their work or life, or it might be experiences such as an exercise set up during a workshop.

All of the final year undergraduates at Warwick Business School take a module called 'Critical Issues in Management'. Based on case studies and syndicate presentations, it aims to help students develop their ability to think critically about complex and ethical issues in business and management. As a seminar tutor, I act as a facilitator, not as a teacher. Some years ago I received this anonymous written feedback from a student in one of my seminar groups: *'This guy knows nothing'*.

I reflected on the feedback for several days, and concluded that I was okay with it. The feedback reminded me of a statement attributed to Socrates – *'I know that I know nothing'*. (There's no actual record that he said this.) My aim in these seminars is to encourage the students to think – critically – not to tell them what I know.

Plato described Socrates as a midwife who helped others to give birth to their ideas. Socrates asked questions of his students, and helped them to explore their answers. My book on coaching, *Don't Just Do Something, Sit There* (Thomson, 2009), was translated into Chinese. The translator picked up the notion of Socratic questioning in the title of the Chinese text, which translates back as *Modern Midwifery: The Art of Coaching*. We might regard Socrates as the first non-directive coach!

In an article entitled 'Using Socratic Questioning in Coaching', Michael Neenan writes:

> *A Socratic stance in coaching … focuses on asking a person a series of open-ended questions to help promote reflection; this, in turn, is likely to produce knowledge which is currently outside of her awareness and thereby enable*

*her to develop more helpful perspectives and actions in tackling her difficulties. Through this method people are able to reach their own conclusions rather than being told what these should be by the questioner.*

(Neenan, 2009)

In his book *Effective Coaching*, Myles Downey (2003) offers this definition: '*Coaching is the art of facilitating the performance, learning and development of another.*' He goes on to say:

*Facilitating implies that the person being coached has the capacity to think something through for himself, to have an insight or creative idea. It acknowledges that people can learn without being taught.*

(Downey, 2003)

There are many similarities between facilitation of a group event and coaching an individual. Both draw on the skills of listening, questioning and playing back. The coach or facilitator has a responsibility for structuring the process and managing the time. And the coach and the facilitator have choices to make on how much input they will give. My own preference, both as a coach and as a facilitator, is to be primarily non-directive. However, when I'm facilitating a learning and development workshop, I will often open up a PowerPoint file and give an input. (*I do know something!*) On workshops on topics such as assertiveness, time management or coaching skills, I usually combine inputs from me (or through a video) alongside experiential activities and opportunities for reflection. The Kolb cycle of learning from experience is a useful guide here.

I recently designed and facilitated a one-day workshop for one of the administrative departments at the University of Warwick. This was a team-building event rather than a learning and development session. I find it useful to see the two activities of designing and facilitating as complementary. While I am certainly prepared to modify a design in the light of what unfolds during the event itself, the design activity largely takes place before the event. One thing I always do in preparing for a workshop like this is to agree very clear objectives with the head of the department. Any exercises or activities need to be contributing to these objectives. I find that the heart of designing an exercise is often simply to choose two or three open questions for a syndicate or individuals to explore.

This one-day workshop was for a department of 25 people that had recently been formed from the amalgamation of three smaller units. The manager's key objective for the workshop was to help people to get to know each other, and each other's responsibilities, to help promote closer working relationships within the new department. Some of the other factors that guided me in designing the workshop were that I wanted to:

- create a space where people felt okay to share their views;
- have short inputs from the two managers on the key issues facing the department;
- include a number of relevant syndicate exercises where people could explore in smaller groups some of the operational challenges facing the department;
- invite each person to reflect on their own view of change, both in general and in regard to the formation of the amalgamated department;
- use a mix of formats – discussion in the whole group, short inputs from the managers, group work in syndicates, sharing in pairs and individual reflection;
- have a fun and engaging exercise immediately after lunch (each syndicate created a coat of arms and a motto for the department. This was shared using the 'critics' gallery' where the rest of the group first tried to interpret the images on a coat of arms before they were explained);

- end with individual reflections on what each person was taking from the day and what they personally would do as a result;
- finish on time.

We noted above that, during the event itself, the facilitator draws on the skills of listening, questioning and playing back. And, in managing the process and the time, they may need to draw on the skill of voicing – for instance, to ensure that the conversation is not dominated by one or two participants. While the facilitator – like the coach – is not responsible for making decisions, they need to manage the process to encourage the group to make decisions when appropriate.

The following link gives a detailed guide to facilitating a group meeting: https://ctb.ku.edu/en/table-of-contents/leadership/group-facilitation/facilitation-skills/main.

My illustration above is an example of facilitating a team workshop. It was a one-off event. I wasn't coaching the team. In Chapter 20, 'Coaching a team', we noted this useful distinction from David Clutterbuck:

> *The purpose of facilitation is to provide external dialogue management to help the team reach complex or difficult decisions. The purpose of coaching is to empower the team to manage its own dialogue, in order to enhance its capability and performance.*
>
> (Clutterbuck, 2007)

**VIDEO**

In this six-minute video Teresa Lewis explores a variety of Socratic questions that might be used in cognitive behavioural therapy to help a client to evaluate and modify their thinking. She notes that *Socratic dialogue* might be a more helpful term than *Socratic questioning*. Some of the questions she illustrates are:

- What is the evidence your belief is true?
- What is the evidence your belief is not true?
- Is there another point of view?
- Are you misinterpreting the evidence?
- What would you advise a friend who told you something similar?
- What would be good to do now?
- What would you like to do about this situation?

www.youtube.com/watch?v=bfCCnYqL4dE

## References

Clutterbuck, D (2007) *Coaching the Team at Work*. London: Nicholas Brealey.

Downey, M (2003) *Effective Coaching: Lessons from the Coach's Coach*. London: Texere.

Neenan, M (2009) Using Socratic Questioning in Coaching. *Journal of Rational-Emotive and Cognitive-Behavior Therapy*, 27(4): 249–64.

Thomson, B (2009) *Don't Just Do Something, Sit There: An Introduction to Non-directive Coaching*. Oxford: Chandos Publishing.

# Chapter 48: E

## ETHICS

On the LeadershipPlus module on the full-time MBA at Warwick Business School, we spend time inviting the students to explore what the purpose of business is and how to lead ethically in organisations today. I give a short input on three approaches to ethics – three ways of answering the question: *What is the right thing to do?*

- *Deontology* – do whatever the rules or laws say.
- *Consequentialism* – do what will maximise the overall benefit.
- *Virtue ethics* – do what a virtuous person would do.

There are downsides to each of these approaches. In his book *Ethicability*, Roger Steare (2009) sets out the I-RIGHT framework, which brings them together in a model that is a useful guide for assessing different options when faced with an ethical choice:

- Who's Involved?
- What are the Rules? (Deontology)
- Are we acting with Integrity? (Virtue ethics)
- Who is this Good for? (Consequentialism)
- Who could we Harm? (Consequentialism)
- What will stand the test of Time? (Consequentialism and virtue ethics)

A number of coaching bodies, including the European Mentoring and Coaching Council (EMCC) and the Association for Coaching, have agreed a Global Code of Ethics for Coaches, Mentors, and Supervisors. It says:

*The Code is intended as a guidance document rather than a legally binding one that in detail spells out what a member can and cannot do. The Code sets the expectation of best practice in coaching, mentoring, and supervision promoting the development of professional excellence.*

(Global Code of Ethics, 2021, p 1)

While such a guide can set out expectations and guidance, ultimately each of us is responsible for the decisions we take. In his chapter in *Excellence in Coaching*, Allard de Jong (2006) writes that, '*At the end of the day, only you can ensure your integrity in your moment of choice.*'

The Global Code of Ethics discusses a number of issues in regard to working with clients, including contracting and confidentiality. In *Values and Ethics in Coaching*, Iordanou et al (2017) write that:

*Contracting is the part of the coaching relationship that has the potential to minimise several ethical pitfalls that you might fall into as a coach, especially as a novice coach.*

I believe that the key issue in contracting is *clarity* – it's essential that the client knows what they can expect from the coach and also what the coach expects of them. For example, in my own initial conversation with a potential client, I always emphasise that I work primarily non-directively. If they're looking for advice and guidance – which might be an entirely reasonable wish – they need to work with someone else. One of the challenges here is that a client may not really understand how coaching works until they've experienced it.

Contracting may be more complicated when the coach is commissioned, and paid for, by the organisation for whom the coachee works. It may be important to engage in three-way contracting so that the coach, the coachee and the sponsor within the organisation (typically the line manager of the coachee or an HR business partner) are all clear on what is expected. Note that I've used the word *coachee* rather than *client* in that sentence. An interesting issue is who is the client – the person being coached or the organisation that is paying for it? My own practice is to regard the person being coached as my client, but some coaches feel strongly that the organisation is the client. This is a good example of where it's important that you think through what your own stance is.

Turning to confidentiality, I always say to a new client when we are contracting that I will treat everything they tell me as confidential, unless they are doing something dangerous or seriously illegal. I also mention that I may discuss things with my own supervisor, who in turn will treat this in confidence. I've never had to break confidentiality because the client was doing something dangerous or illegal. One possibility is that the danger is to themselves – their situation might make me concerned that they may attempt suicide. I work as a volunteer with the Samaritans, and I often need to ask a caller if they are thinking of suicide. I would similarly ask a coaching client about this if I was concerned. And I would explicitly ask them about other sources of support they might draw upon. We'll talk about boundaries and referral in a moment.

Confidentiality is also more complicated when an organisation is sponsoring the coaching arrangement. The sponsor might expect feedback from the coach on, for example, how much progress the client is making in regard to issues that have been discussed in the three-way contracting. My own practice is that I won't share anything with the organisation without the explicit permission of the coachee. But other coaches take the view that they will give feedback to the organisation. Again, this is a situation where you have a decision to make on what is the right thing to do. And your answer might be, '*It depends*.'

The Global Code of Ethics also discusses excellent practice. Members (of the EMCC or Association for Coaching, for example) are expected to engage in ongoing supervision and continuing professional development. The Code also says:

> *Members will operate within the limit of their professional competence. Members should refer the client to a more experienced or suitably qualified practicing member where appropriate.*
>
> (Global Code of Ethics, 2021, p 9)

This is about boundaries. As we discussed in Chapter 2, 'Boundaries', there are two aspects to boundaries. First, as the Code says, a coach needs to work within the boundary of their *competence*. For example, I am not an accredited counsellor and, although there is overlap between counselling and coaching, I am not qualified to act as a counsellor. Second, there is a boundary of *appropriateness*. So, for example, even if I were an accredited counsellor, it would not be *appropriate* for me to act as a counsellor with the fellow members of staff at the University of Warwick whom I'm coaching. If I think a client needs, for example, to see a counsellor then it's important that I raise this with the client, encouraging them to seek the appropriate support. I have at times continued to coach a client who at the same time was receiving counselling support elsewhere.

Iordanou et al offer this interesting thought in regard to values and ethics for a coach:

> *As a practitioner, if you catch yourself worrying over specific decisions you have made in your practice, this is generally wonderful news. A right level of worry is indicative of your commitment to your clients and your will to provide them with a service that is right and appropriate for them.*
>
> (Iordanou et al, 2017)

REFLECTIVE **TASK**

You might like to take some time to make notes on your own position in regard to some of the ethical issues that may arise in your coaching practice.

- What factors guide you in choosing where to operate on the directive to non-directive spectrum?
- What is your stance in regard to confidentiality? How might this change if there is a third party commissioning the coaching?
- Regarding boundaries, what areas might arise that you would regard as beyond the boundary of your work as a coach? If an issue beyond the boundary arises, what will you do?
- What else will you cover in contracting with a new client?

## References

de Jong, A (2006) Coaching Ethics: Integrity in the Moment of Choice. In Passmore, J (ed) *Excellence in Coaching* (pp 191–202). London: Kogan Page.

Global Code of Ethics (2021) Global Code of Ethics For Coaches, Mentors, and Supervisors. [online] Available at: https://emccuk.org/Common/Uploaded%20files/Policies/Global_Code_of_Ethics_EN_v3.pdf (accessed 7 September 2022).

Iordanou, I, Hawley, R and Iordanou, C (2017) *Values and Ethics in Coaching.* London: Sage.

Steare, R (2009) *Ethicability: How to Decide What's Right and Find the Courage to Do It*. London: Roger Steare Consulting Limited.

# Chapter 49: D

## DEBATE AND DIALOGUE

Debate is something that we're all familiar with. It's the nature of the conversations in Parliament, in courts of law and in negotiations between management and trade unions. In a debate I will defend my position and attack yours. Debate is adversarial. It is about winning and losing. And there are situations where it's entirely appropriate.

In his book *Dialogue and the Art of Thinking Together*, Bill Isaacs (1999) writes that *'dialogue is a conversation in which people think together in a relationship'*. He says that dialogue is

> *a way of taking the energy out of our differences and channelling it toward something that has never been created before. It lifts us out of polarization and into a greater common sense, and is thereby a means for accessing the intelligence and coordinated power of groups of people.*

(Isaacs, 1999)

In a dialogue, certainty is replaced by curiosity, and criticism is replaced by creativity. Table 49.1 highlights how the nature of the conversation is very different in a debate or a dialogue.

**Table 49.1 Differences between debate and dialogue**

|  | Debate | Dialogue |
|---|---|---|
| **Listening** | • Accept little at face value<br>• Listen to challenge others' views<br>• Listen critically for errors or flawed logic<br>• Apply judgement<br>• Talk more than you listen<br>• Plan your rebuttal – wait to talk | • Accept what is said at face value as true for others<br>• Hear others' views as a chance to deepen understanding of them<br>• Listen for their story<br>• Suspend judgement<br>• Listen more than you talk – allow silence<br>• Reflect instead of react – allow the conversation to evolve |
| **Inquiring** | • Interrogate the other person and their views<br>• Ask questions that support your perspective and challenge the other person's perspective | • Ask questions to understand more about the other person's views<br>• Explore assumptions – yours and others' |
| **Voicing** | • Assert and justify your position<br>• Describe gaps in the other person's thinking<br>• Defend your assumptions as being the truth<br>• Say what you think is expected – speak from your role | • Describe your reality and invite others to describe theirs<br>• Speak with your authentic voice – your true thoughts<br>• Acknowledge feelings where appropriate<br>• Acknowledge your contribution to the situation |

In his book *The Fifth Discipline*, Peter Senge (1990) summarises three conditions that are necessary for dialogue.

1. All participants must suspend their assumptions. This does not mean throwing out our assumptions. Rather, we are aware of our assumptions and hold them up for examination. If we hold tightly to our assumptions, this blocks the flow of dialogue.
2. All participants must regard one another as colleagues. This does not mean that we all agree or share the same views. It's easy to feel collegial when everyone agrees. Rather, we regard our 'adversaries' as 'colleagues with different views'. This helps to create a positive tone and a degree of safety, which can help to offset the vulnerability and risk that engaging in dialogue may bring.
3. There must be a facilitator who manages the process. Especially in the early stages, the facilitator helps the participants to avoid slipping out of dialogue into debate. They also help the participants to take responsibility for what is happening. And, when appropriate, they may move the conversation on. As a team becomes more experienced in dialogue, the role of the facilitator becomes less essential.

Senge (1990) writes:

*The artistry of dialogue lies in experiencing the flow of meaning and seeing the one thing that needs to be said now.*

In his book, Isaacs (1999) describes four types of silence that might happen in a dialogue.

1. A silence might be *socially awkward* or *strange*, with people feeling uncomfortable.
2. A silence might be *tense* or *conflictual*, where people who disagree are suspicious of why the other person isn't speaking.
3. A silence might be *thoughtful*, where people are reflecting and listening for new possibilities.

4. A silence might be *sacred*. '*The wisdom of the wider group takes precedence of the chatter of the individual*' (Isaacs, 1999).

Isaacs also describes two senses of time, *kronos* and *kairos*. *Kronos* is the sense of time that most of us experience every day. Many of us have it on our wrist or smart phone, and feel that we need to manage it. *Kairos* is '*the time of the seasons, of the moment*' (Isaacs, 1999). We have an inherent awareness of natural cycles and rhythms, and can appreciate when the time is right for something. As a dialogue deepens, *kronos* gives way to *kairos*. Isaacs writes:

> *People become quite reflective and aware of the conversation as taking place in time, but also lose track of it and begin listening for the sense of meaning that is unfolding.*
>
> (Isaacs, 1999)

In Chapter 46, 'Gestalt coaching', we noted that the coach is hoping to create a dialogue with the client that is characterised by what the philosopher Martin Buber called *I–Thou* interactions. That is, where the coach and client engage with each other in open, mutually respectful ways without seeking to impose their will on the other person. In their chapter on Gestalt coaching in the *Handbook of Coaching Psychology*, Julie Allan and Alison Whybrow write that:

> *Through dialogue the coach encourages the coachee to uncover assumptions and patterns for themselves. The coachee's awareness of how they use language is raised and they are encouraged to use language that reflects their control over themselves and identifies their responsibility for their thoughts, feelings and actions.*
>
> (Allan and Whybrow, 2007)

In my role as a mediator, I am hoping that the participants will engage in a dialogue rather than a debate. In my initial one-to-one conversations, if I get a sense that either or both of the parties is certain that they're right and that there's nothing they themselves need to change, I feel less hopeful that in the joint session they will be able to create a way forward that they're genuinely satisfied with. On the other hand, when mediation is working, the participants are encountering each other in a powerful way, sharing vulnerabilities, expressing emotions, appreciating each other, and disclosing what they really need. There are times when I simply sit back and listen as they speak honestly, powerfully and directly to each other.

---

**VIDEO**

In this three-minute video, Heather Miller Rubens, executive director of the Institute for Islamic, Christian and Jewish Studies, reinforces and expands upon many of the above points on the differences between debate and dialogue: www.youtube.com/watch?v=BHnmysaDuNY

---

## References

Allan, J and Whybrow, A (2007) Gestalt Coaching. In Palmer, S and Whybrow, A (eds) *Handbook of Coaching Psychology* (pp 133–59). London: Routledge.

Isaacs, W (1999) *Dialogue and the Art of Thinking Together*. New York: Currency Doubleday.

Senge, P (1990) *The Fifth Discipline: The Art and Practice of the Learning Organization*. New York: Currency Doubleday.

# Chapter 50: C

## COGNITIVE BEHAVIOURAL COACHING

Cognitive behavioural therapy, or CBT, is now widely used within the NHS to treat conditions such as anxiety and depression. The NHS website offers this clear overview of CBT.

> CBT is based on the concept that your thoughts, feelings, physical sensations and actions are interconnected, and that negative thoughts and feelings can trap you in a vicious cycle.
>
> CBT aims to help you deal with overwhelming problems in a more positive way by breaking them down into smaller parts.
>
> You're shown how to change these negative patterns to improve the way you feel.
>
> Unlike some other talking treatments, CBT deals with your current problems, rather than focusing on issues from your past.
>
> It looks for practical ways to improve your state of mind on a daily basis.
>
> (NHS, 2019)

Coaching isn't therapy. However, similar ideas underpin a cognitive behavioural approach to coaching.

As the name suggests, a cognitive behavioural approach works both at a cognitive and at a behavioural level. If there are no issues in how the client is thinking, then a simpler, behavioural approach – using the GROW model, for example – is all that is needed. In their chapter in *The Complete Handbook of Coaching*, Helen Williams, Nick Edgerton and Stephen Palmer (2010) write that, *'There is no need to focus on psychological aspects if a simple problem-solving model will suffice.'*

In his chapter in *Excellence in Coaching*, Michael Neenan writes that:

> What often blocks the way [to achieving their goals] are the coachee's self-limiting/defeating thoughts and beliefs (eg, 'I'm not good enough'), counterproductive behaviours (eg, procrastination) and troublesome emotions (eg, prolonged anxiety). Cognitive behavioural coaching (CBC) helps coachees to identify, examine and change such thoughts and beliefs, develop productive behaviours and become more skilled at emotional management.
>
> (Neenan, 2006)

He goes on to list seven *performance-interfering thoughts* and *self-limiting beliefs* that clients often have.

1. All or nothing thinking – viewing events in either/or terms.
2. Overgeneralisation – drawing sweeping conclusions on the basis of a single incident or insufficient evidence.
3. Mental filter – only the negative aspects of a situation are noticed.
4. Catastrophising – assuming the worst and, if it occurs, your inability to deal with it.
5. Musts and shoulds – rigid rules that you impose on yourself and others.
6. Fallacy of fairness – believing in a just world.
7. Perfectionism – striving for standards that are beyond reach or reason.

The cognitive behavioural coach will invite the client to explore how realistic their limiting thoughts and beliefs are, to identify alternative and more useful ways of viewing things and to act or experiment on the basis of their revised thinking. You might regard this as raising awareness and encouraging responsibility.

One of the key frameworks used in cognitive behavioural coaching is the ABCDE model.

- **A**ctivating event.

- **B**eliefs and perceptions about this event.

- **C**onsequences – cognitive, emotional, behavioural, physical or interpersonal.

- **D**isputing of self-limiting beliefs.

- **E**ffective and new ways of thinking and behaving.

The ancient Stoic philosopher Epictetus said that, '*People are disturbed not by things, but by the views which they take of them.*' The activating event (A) does not automatically produce the consequences (C). Rather, it the mental processing of A via the client's belief system (B), which leads to C. If a client's thinking or beliefs (B) are irrational or self-limiting, then the coach will dispute (D) these. The intention is to help the client to develop new and more effective ways of thinking and behaving (E).

As an illustration, imagine that a client is feeling very anxious about a presentation they're due to give next week. In conversation with the coach, they realise that what they're most nervous about is being asked a question that they don't know the answer to. They find themself lying awake at night thinking about how embarrassed they'd be. They become irritable at home, and lose their appetite. A host of consequences have followed. Now, if A really did cause C, then everyone who has to give a presentation next week would suffer these consequences. The coach might help the client to make notes that are a more realistic way of thinking, perhaps along the following lines.

- I am very knowledgeable about this subject, and I will prepare thoroughly for the presentation, so I will be able to answer most questions.
- It is true that I may be asked a question that I don't know the answer to.
- If I am asked such a question, I will thank the speaker, say I don't know the answer and promise to find out and get back to them.
- Most people won't remember that this happened anyway.

I find that a common issue that clients bring to me in coaching involves a lack of confidence. A cognitive behavioural approach may help some clients to address this. However, lack of confidence or low self-esteem may run very deep within a client. In some cases this might manifest as impostor syndrome, which we discussed in an earlier chapter. It's important that the coach is clear about boundaries and the depth at which they can operate safely, ethically and effectively. Some clients may need to work with a counsellor or therapist to address a deep-seated lack of confidence.

It is usual in cognitive behavioural coaching to agree with the client what they will do before the next session to practise new ways of thinking or behaving. These task assignments are a large part of the work of cognitive behavioural change. Breaking unhelpful ways of thinking or changing well-established beliefs takes time and requires commitment from the client.

A task assignment might be some form of behavioural experiment. For example, a client who is nervous about speaking up in meetings might set themself the challenge of saying one thing early on in each of the meetings they have scheduled for the coming fortnight. They might also make notes to capture what happened and how they thought or felt. They could also use scaling from one to ten to summarise their experience.

At the next session the coach will review with the client how they got on. The point of the review is not to judge success or failure, but rather to help the client to identify what they've learnt and what they will continue to do. This is akin to helping the client to move around the cycle of learning from experience.

**VIDEO**

In this five-minute video Ted Bradshaw talks through a practical technique based on the idea of a continuum of behaviours to help a client to change a fixed or rigid pattern of behaviour: www.youtube.com/watch?v=CY9WBagy2OA

## References

Neenan, M (2006) Cognitive Behavioural Coaching. In Passmore, J (ed) *Excellence in Coaching* (pp 91–105). London: Kogan Page.

NHS (2019) Overview – Cognitive Behavioural Therapy. [online] Available at: www.nhs.uk/mental-health/talking-therapies-medicine-treatme nts/talking-therapies-and-counselling/cognitive-behavioural-therapy-cbt/overview/ (accessed 26 September 2022).

Williams, H, Edgerton, N and Palmer, S (2010) Cognitive Behavioural Coaching. In Cox, E, Bachkirova, T and Clutterbuck, D (eds) *The Complete Handbook of Coaching* (pp 37–53). London: Sage.

# Chapter 51: B

## BEING A COACH

In this chapter we explore the idea of *being* a coach, rather than *doing* coaching, drawing on the views of a number of authors. The distinction is highlighted in this extract from Christian van Nieuwerburgh's book *An Introduction to Coaching Skills*:

> To become a coach requires three areas of learning ... a set of skills, a clear process and a 'coaching way of being'. The first two (the skills and the process) can be taught, and often form the basis of short training courses on coaching. I would argue, however, that simply understanding the skills and following a process will not guarantee successful outcomes. They allow a person to 'do' coaching. The third element is the most influential. Ironically, this element, which I shall refer to as a 'coaching way of being' cannot be taught. Having said that, the most effective coaches have a deep understanding of all three elements.
>
> (van Nieuwerburgh, 2017)

Drawing on the person-centred approach of Carl Rogers that we looked at in Chapter 4, '*Don't Just Do Something, Sit There*', van Nieuwerburgh lists a set of ideal attributes which a coach can aspire to as a '*coaching way of being*'. He suggests that the most effective coaches:

- are humble;
- are confident in their ability as coaches;
- care about people;

- believe that their coachees will achieve more of their potential;
- treat others with respect;
- have integrity;
- demonstrate intercultural sensitivity.

In *The Coaching Manual*, Julie Starr has a chapter entitled 'Becoming a Coach'. She writes:

> *if you want to be frequently engaged in coaching, as an activity, then you will benefit from having your own personal sense of 'being a coach'. It's as though part of your identity (who you think you are) is a coach. Over time, this aspect of who you are develops; you know you're a coach and for you to coach others is a natural form of self-expression. This self-concept will sit alongside other aspects of your identity, e.g. a mother, father, partner, financial advisor, police officer, doctor, etc. When part of your identity includes being 'a coach' it will strengthen and support your ability to coach others. During coaching conversations, your confidence and natural ability is what sustains you, as well as skills, principles and operating beliefs, of course. When you have the inner sense of alignment that comes with being a coach, your confidence, your surety and your energy will all flow more naturally.*
>
> (Starr, 2011)

Becoming a coach is a journey, a fascinating and rewarding journey. It's also a journey without an end – an experienced, competent and confident coach continues to reflect upon and refine their practice. This is one of the key functions of supervision.

In her book *Coaching Presence*, Maria Iliffe-Wood concludes with a final chapter entitled 'A Journey of Self-discovery'.

She emphasises the importance of regularly practising your skill, of supervision, and of developing your own style. She writes:

*Typically coaches are taught skills, but over time how these were taught and how you actually use them become very different: coaches start to develop their own approaches. You are no longer learning a profession, you are developing your art. Any new learning that you take on board will enable you to keep on developing in your own unique way.*

(Iliffe-Wood, 2014)

In his book *Relational Coaching*, Erik de Haan offers ten commandments for an executive coach. His final commandment is *'Don't worry too much about the specific things you are doing'* (de Haan, 2008). He adds:

*If you share the assumption that it is not about the specific things you say or do, you also become more relaxed as a coach about retaining and contributing recollections and suggestions ... You learn to pay more attention to what is actually going on here and now in this coaching relationship.*

(de Haan, 2008)

In his book *Effective Coaching*, Myles Downey discusses the idea of the inner game and some of the interferences that can get in the way of coaching well. One of these is *'Trying to get it right'*. While he advocates a primarily non-directive approach, he writes, *'I need to make sure that we don't get too precious about non-directive coaching. To do so introduces a significant interference'* (Downey, 2003). He adds a postscript:

*Having an insight into one's inner game, one's own uniqueness with all that goes with it balanced with the skills and models of the outer game, is essential to effective coaching.*

(Downey, 2003)

In the concluding chapter of his book *The Coaching Relationship in Practice*, Geoff Pelham (2016) writes that each of us *'puts our own signature'* on our work as a coach. He adds:

*Our signature is the gathering-up of the strands of our lives into a particular 'way of being' – a 'presence', a distinctive, recognisable 'style' that we bring to every activity, coaching included.*

(Pelham, 2016)

Coaching is both a practical skill and an art. In this chapter I'm suggesting that, as you gain more experience and confidence as a coach, you may move beyond skill to art, beyond *doing coaching* to *being a coach*. The skills – such as listening to understand and asking open questions – and tools such as the GROW model remain relevant. But they are more in the background. I've noticed over recent years that I draw much more on my intuition, often asking a question, sharing a metaphor or suggesting an exercise that has popped into my head. I do check in with myself before doing this, but these days I'm more likely trust myself and what I'm thinking or feeling as a conversation is unfolding.

Coaching is also a privilege. Spending your time – and perhaps being paid for – helping others to address their concerns, enhance their performance or realise their potential can bring meaning and fulfilment to you as a coach.

---

**REFLECTIVE TASK**

Geoff Pelham suggests that each of us puts our own signature on our work as a coach. Make some notes in response to this question: *What is your coaching signature?*

# References

de Haan, E (2008) *Relational Coaching: Journeys Towards Mastering One-to-One Learning*. Chichester: John Wiley.

Downey, M (2003) *Effective Coaching: Lessons from the Coach's Coach*. London: Texere.

Iliffe-Wood, M (2014) *Coaching Presence*. London: Kogan Page.

Pelham, G (2016) *The Coaching Relationship in Practice*. London: Sage.

Starr, J (2011) *The Coaching Manual*. Harlow: Pearson.

van Nieuwerburgh, C (2017) *An Introduction to Coaching Skills*. London: Sage.

# Chapter 52: A

## ACCEPTANCE AND COMMITMENT COACHING

In Chapter 50, 'Cognitive behavioural coaching', we looked at how a coach might work with a client to help them to *change* their thoughts or beliefs in order to help them address effectively their problems. Another approach, called acceptance and commitment coaching, in contrast, seeks to help a client to *accept* rather than change their thoughts and feelings, and nevertheless commit to achieving their goals. Both approaches have their background in therapy. In this chapter we look at some of the key ideas in acceptance and commitment (AC) coaching.

If a cognitive behavioural approach can be summarised, in the words of Epictetus, as *'People are disturbed not by things, but by the views which they take of them'*, then an acceptance and commitment approach might be summarised in these words:

> *People are disturbed not by things, nor by the views which they take of them. Rather, it is how they deal with things which shapes their quality of life and personal effectiveness.*

In their chapter in *Mastery in Coaching*, Tim Antiss and Rich Blonna write:

> *The goal of AC coaching is to help clients increase their psychological flexibility – a state characterized by being*

*clear about and living in harmony with one's values, spending time in the present moment, defusing and gaining separation from thoughts, accepting unwanted, unpleasant and unhelpful feelings and sensations and cultivating the perspective of the observing self.*

(Antiss and Blonna, 2014)

Let's explore some of the key terms in that paragraph. In his book *A Liberated Mind: The Essential Guide to ACT*, Steven Hayes, one of the founders of ACT, writes:

*Psychological flexibility is the ability to feel and think with openness, to attend voluntarily to your experience of the present moment, and to move your life in directions that are important to you, building habits that allow you to live life in accordance with your values and aspirations. It's about learning not to turn away from what's painful, instead turning toward your suffering in order to live a life full of meaning and purpose.*

(Hayes, 2019)

Helping a client to clarify and live in harmony with their *values* is a key idea in ACT. Values are what's most important to us. We choose our values. Values are different from goals. We can ask of a goal, '*Am I done yet?*' We can't say this of a value. Antiss and Blonna (2014) write:

*AC coaches help their clients to see how clarifying and living more fully in harmony with their values can help them to flourish as a human being, to live the kind of life they want for themselves, and to reach their potential.*

They go on to say that:

*Many emotions and feelings have a past or future orientation – for instance sadness, regret, anger, shame, guilt, bitterness and hurt tend to be 'backwards looking' emotions, while anxiety, fear and dread tend to be 'forward oriented' emotions.*

(Antiss and Blonna, 2014)

Hence an AC coach will encourage a client to spend more time in contact with the *present moment* – to be *mindful*. Four aspects of mindful moments are as follows.

1. They focus on the present moment.
2. They are non-judgemental, accepting the present moment for what it is.
3. They are non-verbal. Adding speech to describe the present moment adds a level of interpretation and is one step removed from the here and now.
4. They are non-conceptual. During mindful moments nothing gets figured out, worked on, analysed or solved.

An AC coach encourages a client to take the perspective of the *observing self*. Antiss and Blonna (2014) write:

*The 'observing self' can be considered a kind of viewing or observation platform where the client can go to help them 'defuse' or 'disentangle' themselves from unhelpful, unwanted or unpleasant thoughts and feelings, and increase their freedom to act in a more values consistent manner.*

So, for example, the coach might invite the client to focus on their breathing or to notice the sounds in the room, and then to notice what they're noticing.

Another key idea in AC coaching is *experiential avoidance*. Much of what we experience inside our minds and bodies is unhelpful, unwanted, uncomfortable or painful. It is natural to want to avoid or reduce these experiences. An AC coach helps a client to reframe what needs to change. Antiss and Blonna (2014) write:

> *The AC coach helps the client to see that it is not their unwanted experiences per se that are the main cause of their frustration, difficulty, struggle or dissatisfaction, but rather the strategies and tactics they have been using to avoid or attempt to control or reduce these experiences, troubling thoughts and painful emotions.*

A final concept to consider is the idea of *workability*. Whereas a cognitive behavioural coach might challenge a client to assess how realistic a belief is, an AC coach will invite them to consider how helpful or *workable* a belief or coping strategy is. They might, for example, ask the client – with empathy and compassion rather than judgement – to what extent a thought, belief or action is helping them to achieve the life they want to lead.

To sum up, acceptance and commitment coaching seeks to help a client to accept their thoughts and feelings (even when these are unwanted, unpleasant or unhelpful), to clarify and live in harmony with their values, and to commit to achieving their goals. An acronym that encapsulates the Acceptance and Commitment Therapy (ACT) model is ACT.

- **A**ccept your thoughts and feelings and be present.

- **C**hoose a valued direction.

- **T**ake action.

You might be interested in finding out more about the approach, or you might simply want to assimilate one or two of the key ideas discussed above into your own practice.

**READING AND VIDEO**

The link below takes you to a note by Rebecca Wright on Acceptance and Commitment Therapy. The link also includes a four-minute video where the psychotherapist Jimi Katsis gives an overview of ACT: www.counselling-directory.org. uk/acceptance-and-commitment-therapy.html#whatisact

## References

Antiss, T and Blonna, R (2014) Acceptance and Commitment Coaching. In Passmore, J (ed) *Mastery in Coaching* (pp 253–81). London: Kogan Page.

Hayes, S (2019) *A Liberated Mind: The Essential Guide to ACT.* London: Vermillion.

# INDEX